THE Shirley GOODE KITCHEN

SHIRLEY GOODE

Brenda...
5/2/86

BRITISH BROADCASTING CORPORATION

This book accompanies the BBC Television series *The Goode Kitchen*, first broadcast on BBC1 from January 1986. The series was produced by Erica Griffiths.

Published to accompany a series of programmes prepared in consultation with the BBC Continuing Education Advisory Council.

Cover photographs by S. Jeffrey Binns,
Ivanhoe Studios Ltd
Illustrations by Tony Spaul
Home economist: Moya Maynard

This book is set in 10/11pt Gill Light
Photoset on Linotron 202 by
Tradespools Ltd, Frome, Somerset
Printed in England by
Cox and Wyman Ltd, Reading, Berkshire.
Cover originated and printed by
The Malvern Press, London E8.

First published 1986
Published by the British Broadcasting Corporation
35 Marylebone High Street, London W1M 4AA
ISBN: 0 563 21200 4

CONTENTS

1
WHERE THE MONEY GOES

One day I was pushing my trolley round the supermarket…(well, you have to begin a book somewhere)…anyway, there I was with my trolley noticing that, of course, prices had gone up again. Not everything, just the odd thing here and there, but it was enough to start me thinking. With a family to feed, I'd been in charge of the household catering for years. Yet I always seemed to be on the losing end – how, I wondered, did professional caterers manage? Did they have any tips I could profit from? Need I always be an amateur in my own kitchen?

Naturally, I've always known exactly how much money I spend on food each week – when you haven't much money this isn't difficult to work out because you tend to spend it all. But this wasn't enough. I then discovered three things:

- A professional caterer will always buy the best ingredients at a price as low as possible.
  (So what – so do I.)
- When the food is prepared and cooked, there has to be little or no wastage.
  (Well …. I do try.)
- Whether he follows a recipe or invents his own, he knows to the penny just how much the ingredients will cost.
  (To the penny? You must be joking! And anyway what's the point?)

Oh well, I thought, perhaps it's worth a try. After all a professional wouldn't stay in business if it didn't pay. So I started to apply the professional methods of costing in my own kitchen and really look at what I was doing. This is how it works.

Costing the professional way

The trick is to know the cost not just of the whole item but of the smallest amount you're likely to need – for example, 1oz (25g) of flour or cheese, or one egg. The best way is to work it out once and write it on the packet or container, and then to update it once or twice a year to keep pace with those ever-increasing prices. Flour is easy to remember – as long as the price of a 3.3lb (1.5kg) bag doesn't exceed 53p, it won't cost more than 1p per 1oz (25g). Once you know the exact cost of ingredients you can look at any recipe and work out if it could be made more cheaply. Don't ignore the economical recipes – you can even save a few pence when making a pancake batter if, instead of fresh milk, you substitute dried milk and water. There's absolutely no difference in the end result but it does save money. And that's why professionals cost things out.

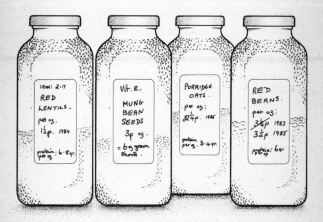

Don't think it's for you? I didn't like the idea either. But before you reject it altogether, here are some games you can play – some challenges you can set yourself. I found these fun to do and I made some amazing discoveries.

- Allow yourself 50p, and see how much you can make for it using your own selection of ingredients.
- Find out the price of a ready-made item – say, a sponge flan – then at home gather together the ingredients for a sponge to the same value. See how much more you can make. (You should be able to make not only the flan, but a Swiss roll and several small cakes as well.)
- Go through your cookery books and cost out various versions of the same recipe – say, chilli con carne – to see which is the best value for money. See if you can improve on it.

Understanding where the money goes is the first step to saving it.

How much do you throw away?

Let's face it – we are a throw-away society. It's the only way manufacturers can be sure of staying in business. Packaging, processing and advertising are all included in the cost of anything we buy. This applies particularly to foods where the actual ingredients represent only a fraction of the price. So, where possible, prepare more at home where *you* have complete control over the ingredients.

Admittedly *some* convenience foods are a worthwhile buy – I use quite a few because saving time is important too – but you need to discover for yourself which ones really are worth it. Don't believe everything the manufacturers tell you. *They* know you can make it yourself quite easily and far more cheaply, but they're certainly not going to let on.

It's not only paper and cans that we throw away – quite a lot of it is food. There was a time when my bin was full of vegetable peelings and outer leaves and the odd meat bone the dog hadn't snaffled first. Now I use these to make soups and stocks. After all, I paid hard-earned money for them and they contain a lot of good food value, so I'd be a fool to throw them all away.

Every time I can serve something 'free', it's one less thing to buy.

The best ingredients

I discovered another secret which I'll pass on to you. Keep it under your hat, though. Food manufacturers haven't yet cottoned on to the idea of charging us extra for food which is nutritionally better for us. So, it's always possible to eat not only cheaply but healthily.

But what is healthy these days? Over the years many of our basic foods have been scrutinised and found to be bad for us for one reason or another. Then lo and behold there's a complete turnaround and it's OK to eat some of them after all. Take bread, for example. When I was younger and worrying about my figure, it was fashionable to refuse to eat bread because we thought it was fattening. Now we know it's not the bread but all the butter and jam we put on it which makes it fattening. We are being positively encouraged to eat more of the stuff – as long as it has a respectable fibre content, of course. So no wonder we're all confused.

There's a growing interest in healthy eating. More and more people are eating fewer fatty foods and more fibre, and several supermarkets have begun to give nutritional information on their own-brand products. But the very best nutrition comes from food that is grown naturally and is un-processed, and the more fresh foods we eat the better. Putting the costing into practice you'll discover that it's also very economical to do as little as possible to food between its source and your plate. Perhaps we'd all have been converted sooner if they'd told us that in the first place.

Essential protein needn't be expensive, and there's no difference in food value whether you buy lean stewing meat or a prime cut. Fish and chicken can cost less per serving than many other meats, fish being a particularly wholesome food which doesn't contain the harmful 'saturated' fats that you get in red meat. A much cheaper source of protein is found in pulses and grains; things like peas, beans, lentils, wheat and oats. Combined with a little animal protein, they make very cheap but nutritious meals. We don't use them enough.

Vitamins are always available all the year round in fresh fruits and vegetables and if you buy them when they are in season they're always fresher, tastier and cheaper than anything else on the market. Why buy anything else? The simplest way to get all the vitamins you need is to have some fresh fruit and vegetables every day (there's always plenty of choice), and if possible eat them raw or just lightly cooked.

Nature gave us a selection of perfectly good food; she didn't know we'd mess about with it and refine all the goodness out of it. The body is like a furnace with food as fuel. Give it too much of the wrong sort and it will clog up – or, at worst, go out altogether.

Fuel running costs

Fuel costs are high, so it makes sense to look into the running costs of preparing and cooking food. Just as food is sold by the pound or kilogram, so electricity and gas are sold by the unit and the therm. The price of a unit or a therm is shown on your bill.

- If you cook with electricity, one week's meals for a family of four will use roughly 20 units.
- If you cook with gas, the same number of meals will use up $1\frac{1}{2}$ therms.

With all this concern over high fuel costs, it isn't surprising that many people believe buying something ready prepared will save them money.

☆ *Consider this: the cost of buying a can of soup and heating it up comes to about the same as making your own soup and paying for all the fuel needed to cook a whole day's meals.*

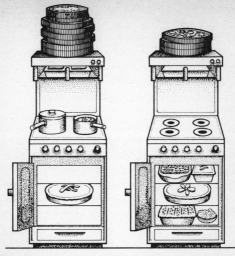

Try to fill the oven when using it by, for example, cooking your vegetables and pudding along with the main meal. You can knock pounds off your fuel bill in this way.

Don't forget that ovens retain heat long after you've turned them off. You've paid for this, so why not use it? Here's a recipe which uses the heat of a cooling oven. It works for either gas or electricity, but you can only do it successfully if the oven has been on at gas mark 5, 375°F (190°C) or higher.

Meringue crunchies
Makes 30–36

2 egg whites (size 3 or 4)
5oz (150g) caster sugar
6oz (175g) crunch – this can be a mixture of anything you've got, e.g. crisp cereal, broken biscuits, muesli, chocolate chips, nuts

Beat the egg whites with the sugar for 3 minutes with an electric whisk until really thick. It will take longer if you're doing it by hand. Fold in the crunchy bits. Line 3 baking sheets with foil and dot with teaspoonsful of the mixture, leaving room for them to spread. Place the baking sheets in the oven before you turn it out. Shut the door, turn off the heat and leave the cookies for at least 8 hours. Don't open the door!

Plain meringues can also be made using this 'free' heat. You can dry out breadcrumbs and cook oatcakes too (for recipe see p.123).

Here are some other ways of saving fuel using different methods of cooking. Not all these gadgets are cheap to buy, but it's worth saving up for them for long-term economy. Remember that if you use a money-saving gadget *regularly*, it very soon pays for itself.

- *Steamer:* If you buy a 'stack' steamer you can use this to cook several things at once, e.g. potatoes in the bottom and carrots and cabbage (cut into small even-sized pieces) in the top.
- *Slow cooker:* A slow cooker (or crockpot) uses very little electricity – about the same as a couple of 60 watt light bulbs. It is an excellent way of producing rich hearty casseroles from the cheaper cuts of meat.
- *Pressure cooker:* A very worth while investment – cooking times are considerably reduced when cooking under pressure, and if you buy one which has more than one compartment you can save even more fuel by cooking more than one thing at once.
- *Microwave oven:* Although a microwave oven means a big initial outlay, it is very cheap to run and, if you use it regularly, will soon repay you by reducing both your fuel bills and the amount of time you spend cooking.

But – and this is the best fuel-saving advice of all – remember that not every part of a meal, even in winter, needs to be hot. Cook only what is necessary and eat as much raw food as you can.

☆ *Ask at your gas and electricity showrooms for leaflets on fuel running costs. Just as with money, once you know where the most fuel is used, the easier it is to save it.*

Shopping

Now this really *is* where the money goes. And before your very eyes too – isn't it amazing how easily it trickles through your fingers into the till. One tip I learnt from the professionals is to concentrate on buying one section of food at a time. It works surprisingly well for me. I divide my food budget into four, setting aside one quarter of my money for each of these four sections:

1 Fish and meat
2 Fruit and vegetables
3 Dairy produce
4 Groceries

Now this probably means revising the way you shop. Before, I used to sail up and down the aisles of the supermarket picking things off the shelves as I came to them. Popping in the odd extra item that caught my eye too. Now I try to concentrate on one section at a time, bearing in mind my allowance. The whole idea is not to *spend* to the last penny the money allocated to each section, but to *save* as much of it as you can. You'll probably find that you'll save easily on some sections – especially dairy produce – and not so easily on others. I use the leftover money to supplement another section or to take advantage of a bargain or economy pack. Or I may put it towards another kitchen gadget – or even a treat!

I also try not to do all my shopping in one place. I'm particularly keen on buying my meat from the local butcher. He can tell you a lot about the quality and cuts of the meat he sells, and he'll give you exactly the amount you need. Unfortunately, fresh fish shops aren't so easily come by although many are opening up again and some supermarkets now have excellent fresh fish counters. Again I try to buy my fish from a knowledgeable fishmonger – he'll know what's in season, what's fresh and even introduce you to new gastronomic experiences!

Shopping lists I always used to think the efficient shopper made a list and stuck to it. I couldn't understand why it never worked for me. Now I find I only need to make a list for Section 4 – groceries. My weekly buys from the dairy section are usually pretty standard so I can remember them, and as all fresh food prices fluctuate according to the weather and the season, it's best to be on the spot before you decide what to buy, and *not* to plan meals ahead before you see what's available.

Supermarkets Even quite small supermarkets usually have something marked down in price. Because of the high standard, even the half-price fresh foods are good value but only buy them if you can *really* use them. If you're shopping for one, there's no point in staggering home on Saturday afternoon with an enormous cut-price pork pie which will be beyond the safe eating date long before you get through it. Ask yourself if you *really* need that bargain – or are you just attracted by the money off.

   Here are some tips about supermarket shopping which I find helpful.

- Read the posters outside the shop to see if something you really want has been reduced.
- Get to know your own supermarket's policy – they all have a system of introducing money-savers and bargains.

- Read the labels on the food you buy – there's a lot to learn. Sell-by dates and eat-by dates are often clearly marked. The packs at the front of the display will probably have a shorter life than the ones at the back – useful to know if you don't want to eat something straight away.
- Collect money-off coupons and use them. Each household receives about £50 worth a year. Swap any you don't need with friends.
- Share large packs with a friend to take advantage of the extra saving.
- Try to shop in season for fish, meat, fruit and vegetables. It's always tastier and cheaper.
- Try not to shop when you're hungry. Large packets of crisps or biscuits will seem just too tempting.
- Check the prices on items at the back of the shelf. There may be something still available at the old price because it's illegal to mark up shelved stock with a new price rise.
- Always pay cash, never by cheque or credit card. It's too easy to slip in those extra things you don't really need.
- Always use a basket when shopping mid-week. The sheer weight of it will prevent you from buying too much.
- Use a calculator to keep a running total as you shop. You'll see immediately if you start overspending.

To make or not to make

That is the question. In other words, am I a failure if I pop down to the shop for something I could perfectly well make at home? No, is the short answer to that. But I do like to know the value of the food I'm buying and one way of finding out is to see what it really costs to make it.

The other day I bought one 1lb 12oz (800g) wholewheat loaf. Then I decided to cost out a recipe for making my own bread. Here's the recipe.

Wholewheat loaf

1lb (450g) wholewheat flour
1lb (450g) strong plain flour
1½oz (40g) lard
1 sachet instant dried yeast powder (see p.137)

Mix the flours together and rub in the lard. Sprinkle over the yeast and stir in approximately 1¼ pints (700ml) hand-hot water with a wooden spoon. The amount of water depends a great deal on the flour you use. You may need slightly more or slightly less to obtain a soft, but not sticky dough. Knead well for 10 minutes and press into two 2lb (1.1kg) greased tins. Leave to rise until the dough reaches the top of the tins. I like to knock the dough out at this point, knead again and leave to rise a second time, as I think the loaf is lighter if it has risen twice. However, you can bake the loaves after the first rise. Bake near the top of the oven at gas mark 7, 425°F (220°C) for 10 minutes. Reduce the heat to gas mark 5, 375°F (190°C) and bake for a further 40 minutes. If you have an electric oven, turn out the heat after 30 minutes. Cool on a wire rack.

Yes, you've guessed it. I made *two* 1lb 12oz (800g) loaves with this recipe for the price of one bought loaf. So – to make or not to make? Find out the costs and then decide whether you'd rather save time or save money.

☆ *You only ever need to pre-heat the oven if the dish takes 20 minutes or less to cook. And don't pre-heat the grill unless you're using it for quick browning.*

Whatever I do I seem to be consumed with guilt. I'm either spending too much money, or not enough and starving the family. I'm trying to make them eat things they don't want simply because I can afford them or I think they're good for them. Why, they constantly ask me, can't we just eat the things we like? And I ask myself that too – they'd all love me a lot more if that's what I gave them. But then I *would* be justified in feeling guilty.

I'd know that I wasn't getting the best value for my money with a constant diet of fish fingers, crisps and chocolate biscuits. But once you've got the money sorted out on the food which is going to do your family the most good, then you'll find you can afford to give them treats.

The whole idea of all this budgeting is not to live on a prison diet, but to be able to afford the best possible ingredients, and that includes the odd luxury too. I can honestly say that as my housekeeping expenditure went down, the standard of living in our house went up. I found it an exciting challenge and still get an enormous amount of satisfaction from creating recipes. After all, we're not given the chance to do that much these days – food manufacturers have done it all for us by presenting us with ready-made meals. They've taken all the fun out of it for us. I think it's time we got that fun back.

2
THE KITCHEN

You don't need a big kitchen to be a good cook. One of the best I know cooks day after day, six months of the year, in a tiny ship's galley, often in the most appalling conditions (I know – I've been there). She has no electrical gadgets to aid her, yet manages to produce hot scones, fresh bread, gorgeous home-made soups and salads throughout the day. Every evening she serves up a three-course gourmet meal for eleven people and hardly ever resorts to canned or convenience foods.

Fortunately, most of us work on a more even keel and with a little more space, but there's no rule that says a kitchen has to be large or fitted with modern units. The kitchen is what you make of it and a great deal of that can be do-it-yourself.

Above all, the kitchen should be a place where you want to be. And considering the amount of love and care that goes into meal preparation, it's your right that you should be in a place worthy of you. A happy cook is a better cook.

Most professional craftsmen have a proper workplace and the right tools for the job, otherwise their work won't be of the highest quality. The family cook has to share her (or his) work room with the rest of the family and is still expected to come up with good quality meals. And yet, although we all know that can be very trying, I think it all helps towards a happy kitchen with children piling in to raid the fridge and the family pet taking over a cosy corner just by the boiler.

As long as the hygiene and safety factors are taken care of, this is just the kind of kitchen I like. Most domestic accidents happen in the kitchen – not surprising when you think of all those knives, choppers, boiling kettles, pans of sizzling oil and electrical gadgets.

So make sure that *your* working area is right for you. Ask yourself some questions:

● Can you see what you're doing?
  If the light is too dim or in the wrong place, it's not only dangerous but you won't enjoy spending long in the kitchen.
● Are your work surfaces cluttered with things?
  If you haven't room to manoeuvre, hot pans are liable to fall off. See if you can get more shelves fixed up to store the extra clutter on – or get rid of some of it!
● Does the room look cheerful and welcoming when you go into it?
  A slap of white paint works wonders and so do cheerful teatowels or posters on the walls.

My kitchen breaks most of the rules. It has no really modern units and relies a great deal on junk shop buys to give it character. My freezer is disguised as a Welsh dresser! I could never afford the real thing and the freezer was an eyesore.

We have no larder and I have a lot of open shelving. There's no law that says everything has to be kept behind closed doors. I find the fashion for fitted kitchens with their serried ranks of blank cupboard doors soul-less and uninspiring. The more you see of your ingredients and equipment, the more you're inspired to use them. And, of course, my windowsill is full of pots of herbs, mustard and cress and other things I'm experimenting with growing. Most of my crockery has been bought at junk shops and white elephant stalls. None of it is worth anything so it doesn't matter if it gets broken. Most of my stainless steel cutlery was won at seaside bingo. Money is spent on the essentials: the tools for the job.

The tools for the job

Just as you don't need a large kitchen to be a good cook, so you don't need a whole battery of tools and gadgets. There's a cheap substitute for virtually everything except knives.

- Use the grill rack to double up as a cake rack.
- Bake cakes in left-over straight-sided biscuit tins.
- Use plastic sweet jars, fruit juice and coffee jars for storage.
- Use plastic ice-cream tubs and yoghurt pots for storage in the fridge or freezer.
- Use a sturdy glass bottle as a rolling pin.
- Use cups or mugs for measures.
- Grow your herbs in clean syrup or treacle tins or yoghurt cartons (remove the lettering with a Brillo pad but leave any patterning on).
- Clear plastic egg cartons can substitute for ice cube trays or for freezing small amounts of things like stock or tomato purée.
- Use empty screw-top jars and bottles (sparkling-drink type) for home-made preserves, vinegars and drinks.
- A heatproof bowl set over a small saucepan works fine as a double boiler.
- Keep plastic and paper bags for re-use.

Eventually, dedicated cooks, especially budget-minded ones, will put their savings towards the proper tools. This makes life easier and every craftsman – and there's no question that cooking *is* a craft – deserves them.

Knives These have to be the best you can afford. Far better to have two good sharp knives than a dozen cheap ones. A vegetable knife (small) and a longer-bladed one should see you through most things. A serrated bread knife is also useful but most *really sharp* kitchen knives can cut through almost anything. You need a steel to keep them sharp – sharpen them every time you use them. Then keep them out of the way. Never in a drawer – this blunts them as well as taking off the tops of fingers. The very best way is on a magnetic rack, where the blade doesn't touch anything rough.

I also wouldn't be without a strong pair of kitchen scissors.

Spatulas, wooden spoons and whisks Flexible spatulas can scrape every last bit out of a bowl so they're really essential for the cost-cutting cook. I keep two sets of wooden spoons, one for sweet, one for savoury. We happen to like curry but not in the custard. A long-handled one is best for jam-making. I prefer flat whisks to balloons as they can double as straining spoons. All these are kept out on the work surface in stone jars bought in junk shops.

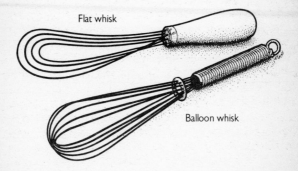

Flat whisk

Balloon whisk

Bowls At least three different sizes. Stainless steel ones are very good, especially for whisking egg whites, but heatproof glass are almost as good. You need one enormous bowl for bread-making, batch-baking and making up drinks.

Pots and pans Again it really pays to get the best you can afford. Anything non-stick also saves on the cost of oiling as well as detergent, but if you invest in non-stick do look after them properly. Three pans should be enough – buy two the same size and one smaller. A large frying-pan, also non-stick, is essential. Get a steamer with a lid to fit your larger pans.

Glass saucepans get very hot so you can cook over a very low heat. They retain the heat so well that the contents bubble away for a time after the heat has been turned out. A really good heavy-weight baking sheet is worth twelve of a cheaper type. I also prefer a non-stick bread tin and flan tin. More baking is ruined by poor tins than bad cooks.

Sieves and strainers These are essential, and it's always worth having at least three different sizes, one of which could be conical as this type makes it easier to control liquids. It's also better to have a colander with one long handle rather than two short ones as this helps to prevent scalds.

A vegetable mill (or *mouli*) is excellent for puréeing fruit and soups. It comes with different-sized discs so you can choose the texture of the food. It gives soups a slightly chunky consistency – much nicer than the totally smooth liquid you get in a liquidiser.

Casseroles At least one deep one for giant stews and one shallow one for pasta-type dishes. This can also double up as a serving dish for salads.

Tin opener A good-quality hand-held version is all you need. Wall-mounted or electric ones are unnecessary. Make sure you clean it well; it's surprising how much gunge gets embedded in the works.

Scales and liquid measures I haven't yet found a set of scales I'm really happy with but I crave the old-fashioned brass balance type. They are the most accurate and you can buy them now with both metric and imperial weights. Expensive but worth saving up for.

Get one heatproof jug for measuring liquids. A measuring cup is essential if you use American recipes.

Graters Mine is ancient but in regular use. Food processors do the job more quickly, but they're for luxury kitchens. I'm also fond of my tiny nutmeg grater – the nutmegs are kept in a box at the top. There's nothing to compare with nutmeg freshly ground. In the past it was common for a housewife to wear a belt with all the necessaries hung around it: scissors, sewing equipment, nutmeg graters and so on. My version would be the grater, small screwdriver, bottle opener, tin opener, measuring spoons and a corkscrew.

Mincer Essential for mincing your own meat so you can be sure it's all lean. Useful too for mincing citrus peel when making marmalade.

Chopping and pastry boards My chopping board, slightly warped, was used by somebody long ago. I like continuity like that. One side I keep for meat (marked MEAT), the other for vegetables. I have a standard wooden pastry board handed down by my mother, but Formica ones are also very good. I'm saving up for the marble slab. Until then my pastry won't improve!

Lemon squeezer The glass or plastic kind is all you need. I saw an electric lemon squeezer in a shop the other day – whatever next! Are we so enfeebled these days we can't even squeeze a lemon?

Potato peeler Useful not only for potatoes but for paring the peel finely from oranges and lemons. Some double up as an apple corer.

Pressure cooker I'm including this in my list of essential equipment even though I know you can manage very well without it. But it saves literally hours of cooking time and I strongly urge you to buy a good cookbook on the subject and learn to love your pressure cooker! You won't regret it.

Electrical equipment None of this is *absolutely essential*, but of course there's no denying it all makes life a lot easier. My mother brought up her family without a single thing in the kitchen she could plug in – now there's very little that hasn't been electrified!

These are the electrical gadgets I find most useful as they save me time and money:

- Liquidiser/coffee grinder
- Electric hand whisk
- Toaster – one which takes thick slices
- Electric kettle
- Slow cooker

Two other electrical gadgets which are undoubted time and money savers are the food processor and microwave oven. Both are expensive, but if you do a lot of cooking and use them regularly, they will pay for themselves in less time than you think.

☆ *It's cheaper to boil water in an electric kettle than on an electric ring. Don't boil more than you need but make sure you always cover the element.*

Cookery books

Everybody should have at least one basic one. If you can't cook, begin with one that teaches you how – *with pictures*. Progress from there.

Cookery books cost money so don't fall for every new one that's published. Very few recipes are brand new so you've probably got them already in another form. But some books are worth it and a thrifty cook should be able to recoup the cost by judicious use of the recipes. It may mean adapting them to make a cheaper version (this is where the costing out counts), but you can learn a lot that way. Following a recipe exactly can be one of the most expensive ways to cook. Everything is carefully listed in weights and measures and new cooks don't usually dare to alter a gram. Experience, however, proves that most recipes (especially savoury ones) are adaptable, and you can add or subtract, give or take a little, depending on what you happen to have on hand at the time of making. Try, though, to keep the total weight the same or that recipe to feed four may end up feeding only two.

You need to be confident. Believe that what you are doing will work and it will – even if it really shouldn't. Otherwise why in the early days did everything I make – exactly by the book – fail, and now I chuck in all sorts of things without weighing and it works!

Many old cookbooks don't list ingredients, they just expect you to add what you have. These are fun to read and you can get some really economical recipes from them. They are usually cheap and can be found by rummaging around in second-hand bookshops.

Eating foods from foreign lands is fairly recent in this country, so ethnic recipe books will be new but well worth buying as many foreign dishes are economical. Unlike us many countries have developed dishes using simple ingredients to an extremely high standard.

Don't forget libraries have a good collection of cookbooks – read them all. If one takes your fancy, try to buy it second-hand.

3
FISH AND MEAT

For as long as I can remember, meat has been the centrepiece of our diet in this country. A good joint of meat on the table meant that not only were we well fed, but that we were able to provide the best for our family. Meat is expensive so it has become almost a status symbol. If we can't afford roast beef for Sunday lunch we tend to feel we have failed in some way.

Of course, the very reverse of this is true – those of us who provide less meat are actually doing our families a favour. Red meat contains a high proportion of saturated fat which is bad for us. If we constantly eat such food, it increases the level of cholesterol in our bloodstream and this clogs up our arteries. Nasty thought. Beef and lamb contain the highest amount of saturated fat, pork is the next highest and lowest of all is poultry. So you see, once again, the cheaper foods turn out to be nutritionally better for you. There is some justice after all! The best news of all is that fish and rabbit are positively good for you, containing a high proportion of fats which help our arteries not to clog up – 'polyunsaturated' fats.

But no one wants to give up something they really like – nor do we need to. There are plenty of ways of eating meat which 'get round' the fat problem so we can still enjoy its wonderful flavour.

Always cut off the visible fat and remove chicken and turkey skin if you're making a casserole or curry. Grill your meat rather than fry it – this only adds to the fat content. Buy your sausages and pies from your butcher and ask him what's in them – better still, make your own using your own lean minced meat. Avoid meat in tins if possible – meat isn't so essential in our diet that we can't find a better basis for a meal than this. But above all, eat more fish!

FISH

I think my husband must have sea water running in his veins – I can't keep him away from it. He dives, he sails and, best of all, he sometimes arrives home with a silvery parcel of the freshest of fresh fish. There's really nothing nicer in the whole world than a fish cooked straight from the sea.

So I've been lucky. But over the last few years, fresh fish has been difficult to come by for many people; my local fishmonger closed years ago. Recently though I've noticed that fresh fish is slowly making a comeback. Best of all, some supermarkets now have a fresh fish counter so it should be possible to find it somewhere in your area. Once you've found your fishmonger, cosset him! He'll order almost anything you want and will take on those rather nasty jobs of beheading and gutting if you can't face them yourself.

Eat your fish as soon as you've bought it. It droops quickly and doesn't like sitting around in the refrigerator. Cooked fresh, it's a little time-bomb of protein, vitamins and minerals and its oils are that OK thing, polyunsaturated! In fact, fish oils are actually good for us and many of the oily fish are also the most nutritious. They're often the cheapest too.

Cooking

One of the worst things you can do is overcook fish. The most foolproof way of cooking all fish is 'en papillote' – a posh way of saying in an envelope. All you do is wrap up the fish loosely but securely in a parcel of foil with a little chopped onion, herbs and a squeeze of lemon juice and bake it in the oven.

☆ *To get more juice from your lemon, place it in a bowl of hot water for 5 minutes, then cut it and squeeze the juice.*

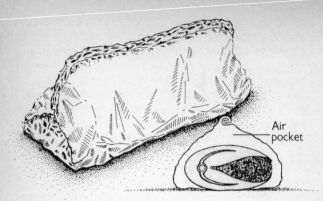

Air
pocket

Fish stock: Fumet de poisson

Sooner or later all this moneysaving means affordable
luxury food, and if I look up a recipe for something
special in the fish line, it's almost a certainty that one of
the ingredients will be fish stock.

So it's worth making a batch to keep ready and
waiting in the freezer for the Big Day. Unfortunately
most frozen fish is already filleted and prepared so
there's little wastage. However, fishmongers have all the
bits. Some may give them away, but even if you have to
pay they're always very cheap and you should find
enough flesh cooks off to use in fish soups (chowders)
and some rice dishes. After all, if a recipe calls for small
bits of fish then why pay for larger pieces, when you
can get them cheap?

All you need for stock are the bones and trimmings
of fish (the heads and tails and fins) which go into a pot
with a small bunch of fresh herbs (parsley, thyme and
bay). Add some sliced onion, the juice of a lemon and
the stalks of a few mushrooms and cover with a blend
of water and white wine. The amount of wine depends
upon how much you can afford, but if you keep wine
concentrate in store you will be sure you can add some.
Simmer for one hour, then strain, cool and freeze.

Captain's chowder

12oz (350g) white fish (e.g. coley, cod, whiting)
15fl oz (400ml) fish stock
4oz (110g) potatoes, peeled
Bacon bits, diced
Cooking oil
1 onion, diced
1 tablespoon plain flour
5fl oz (150ml) milk
Black pepper, freshly ground
Parsley, chives or spring onion tops, chopped

Poach the fish in the stock until it flakes. Remove the skin and bones. Set the stock and flaked fish on one side. Boil the potatoes. In a large pan, fry the bacon in the oil until crisp. Remove with a slotted spoon and drain on kitchen paper. Add the onion to the pan and fry gently till it has softened. Stir in the flour, then gradually pour in the fish stock and milk, stirring all the time. Bring to the boil and cook for 2–3 minutes. Dice the cooked potatoes and add them, with the flaked fish, to the pan. Season and garnish with parsley, chives or spring onion tops. Serve with warm crusty bread.
Note: To make this into a main course, you could add cooked peas and diced carrots along with the potatoes and fish.

Fish sauces
Apart from the classic sauces these three 'cheapies' go very well with fish.

Mustard sauce Using a standard white sauce recipe, blend in 1 teaspoon mustard powder with the flour before adding the liquid.

Tartare sauce Bought or home-made tartare sauce goes further if blended with yoghurt.

Seafood sauce A half-and-half mixture of tomato ketchup and yoghurt is as good a seafood sauce as any you can buy in the bottle.

White fish

White fish contains less than 2% oil and has very lean flesh. The group is enormously varied – there are the round fish, which include cod, coley, (sometimes known as saithe), haddock and whiting, and the flat fish, which tend to be more expensive, e.g. sole, plaice, dab, halibut and brill.

These are the months when these fish should be at their best:

Cod	*June to February*
Coley	*August to February*
Haddock	*May to February*
Whiting	*June to February*
Sole	*May to March*
Plaice	*May to March*
Dab	*September to May*
Halibut	*June to March*
Brill	*June to February*

Cooking Moist cooking is best to prevent the flesh drying out. You can cook it in parcels, or steam it over a pan in which you're cooking the accompanying vegetables. All you do is put the fish with seasonings on a heatproof plate and cover it with another plate. You can also bake it in the oven with a variety of sauces.

☆ *The 10 minute rule. Measure your fish steak or fillet at its thickest point and allow 10 minutes for each inch (double the cooking time if the fish is frozen). Insert a fork – if the fish flakes, then it's done.*

Fish creole

This original New Orleans dish calls for white chunky
fish fillets. As it has to be cut up into bite size pieces
anyway I would plump for fish scraps which always
contain usable pieces. Plan to make this and fish stock at
the same time. Buy extra scraps, take out the best bits
for Fish Creole and use the rest for stock.

12oz (350g) white fish
½oz (10g) butter
Cooking oil
8oz (225g) long grain rice
2 onions, chopped
2 sticks celery, diced
1 green pepper, cut into strips
A squirt of garlic purée
1 can (14oz/400g) tomatoes
Tabasco sauce to taste
3 tablespoons frozen peas

Cut up the fish into bite-size pieces and remove any
bones. In a pan heat the butter with a little oil and stir in
the rice. Cook for a few seconds and add 10fl oz
(300ml) water. Bring to the boil, reduce the heat, cover
and simmer for 10 minutes. Remove from the heat, fluff
the rice with a fork and cover the pan with a clean
cloth. Replace the lid.

Meanwhile, heat a little more oil in a pan. Fry the
onions, celery and pepper gently until tender and stir in
the garlic purée. Add the cut-up fish to the vegetables,
also the tomatoes with their juice, a dash of Tabasco
and the peas. Bring to the boil, reduce the heat and
simmer for 5–10 minutes until the fish is cooked. Serve
with the rice and a salad.

Fatima's fishcakes   *Serves 4*

I like to believe this recipe originated when Fatima saw the sharing of the loaves and fishes. It struck her that you can feed a lot on far less than you think. She decided to go one step further and find a use for the leftovers in the bottom of the baskets.

---

8 slices wholewheat bread
10fl oz (300ml) milk
12oz (350g) fresh white fish, skinned and minced
½ onion, peeled and grated
3 tablespoons fresh parsley, finely chopped
Grated rind of 1 lemon
Black pepper, freshly ground
Wholewheat flour
Cooking oil

Crumb the bread and soak in the milk until all the liquid has been absorbed. Place in a sieve and press gently with a wooden spoon to squeeze out the excess milk. Put the bread into a bowl and mix together with the minced fish, onion, parsley, lemon rind and pepper to taste. Flouring your hands thoroughly, divide mixture into 12 portions.

Shape into flat round cakes about ½ inch (1cm) thick. Place on a floured plate until all are done. They can be frozen at this stage.

To cook, heat the oil in a large frying pan and when hot put in the fish cakes. Reduce the heat to medium and fry for a few moments on each side until crispy and golden. Drain on kitchen paper and serve. How about having them for breakfast with grilled tomatoes?

Note: This recipe works equally well using flaked smoked haddock.

☆ *Cheap oven chips: cut thin chips, brush lightly*
  with sunflower oil and grill, turning once, for 10
  minutes.

Fish and red bean salad   *Serves 4*

Here's a colourful dish which I've re-named 'Grandma's
Jewels' as it's a proper little treasure trove of good
things to eat.

1lb (450g) white fish (e.g. coley, cod, haddock)
8oz (225g) red kidney beans, cooked
8oz (225g) sweet corn, cooked
1 large green pepper, diced

Place the fish in a pan, cover with water and simmer
until cooked. Remove the bones and skin and fork into
flakes. Toss with all the other ingredients. Serve cold
with a lemony dressing (see below), crisp green salad
and hot crusty bread with garlic butter.

It makes you glad to be a Grandma!

Lemony dressing

---

3 tablespoons oil (olive oil is best but if you can't afford
the real thing you can make your own – see p.130)
1 tablespoon lemon juice
Black pepper, freshly ground

Put all the ingredients in a screw-top jar and shake until
well blended.

Koulibiac

This very traditional Russian fish pie should be made
with salmon, but my peasant version works perfectly
well with a mixture of less expensive fish.

Basically Koulibiac is made from a mixture of fresh
chopped vegetables, rice, hard-boiled eggs, herbs and
fish, but between you and me it works just as well using
left-overs as it's all got to be cooked and cooled before
assembling. You don't need to bother with exact

amounts – I just play it by ear – but allow roughly 2–3oz (50–75g) fish and half a hard-boiled egg per person.

A mixture of cooked flaked fish (cod, haddock, tinned mackerel etc)
Cooked onions, carrots, celery, chopped
A few fresh mushrooms, cooked or raw, roughly chopped
Rice (preferably cooked in chicken stock rather than water)
Fresh parsley, chopped
Hard-boiled eggs, finely chopped
Black pepper, freshly ground
Enough shortcrust pastry to wrap it all up
Melted butter

Combine all ingredients except the butter and pastry. Roll out half the pastry, brush with a little melted butter, pile on the filling and drizzle a little more melted butter over the top. Cover with the remaining pastry. Seal the edges, make one or two slits and bake at gas mark 4, 350°F (180°C) until the pastry is golden – about 30 minutes. Serve hot with Mustard Sauce (see p.27) and a green salad.

Eggs Benedict   *Serves 4*
Not all versions of this recipe use fish, but this one does and is all the more tasty and nutritious because of it. Quite substantial enough for a main course, it only takes minutes to prepare. I'm quite hopeless at poaching eggs but find that halved soft-boiled eggs are just as good.

---

4 eggs, gently poached (or soft boiled and shelled)
12oz (350g) white fish, cooked
A squirt of garlic purée
2 tablespoons top of the milk or thick yoghurt
15fl oz (400ml) white sauce
3oz (75g) Cheddar cheese, finely grated

Place the cooked eggs in a bowl of warm water until needed. Mix together the flaked fish, garlic purée and top of the milk or yoghurt with 5fl oz (150ml) of the white sauce. Spread this in an oiled fireproof dish. Arrange the eggs, yolks uppermost, on top of the fish mixture. Stir half the cheese into the remaining white sauce and pour over the eggs and fish mixture. Top with the rest of the cheese and brown under the grill. Serve with toast. This is a good recipe for one person if you reduce the quantities appropriately. It makes a good lunch dish.

Seviche   *Serves 4*

You don't always need to heat fish. Sometimes other ingredients can 'cook' it for you by way of a marinade. Perfect for summer eating, serve Seviche with a crisp salad, crusty bread and a cold bottle of plonk.

1lb (450g) meaty white fish (e.g. coley, cod or haddock)
Juice of 2 lemons
Juice of 1 lime (or a third lemon)
3fl oz (75g) olive oil (home-made, see p.130)
1 teaspoon coriander, freshly ground
Black pepper, freshly ground
2 bay leaves
4oz (110g) small mushrooms

Garnish:
A black olive
Fresh coriander (optional)

Skin the fish and break it into flakes. Place in a shallow dish and cover with the juice of the lemons and the lime. Leave to marinate overnight in the fridge until the fish is opaque.

Heat the oil gently in a pan with the ground spices and bay leaves. Infuse for a few moments – do not boil.

Leave to cool and remove the bay leaves. Drain the fish and cover with a layer of sliced mushrooms. Pour the spicy oil over everything and toss gently. Garnish with stoned and sliced black olives and – if you've got them – fresh coriander leaves.

Seafood pasta   *Serves 4*

1lb (450g) noodles, e.g. tagliatelle (a mixture of green and white is nice)
1lb (450g) fish: a mixture of cod, coley and smoked haddock is good
Cooking oil
1 onion, chopped
Grated rind and juice of 1 lemon
10fl oz (300ml) chicken stock
1 heaped teaspoon French mustard
Black pepper, freshly ground
1 teaspoon cornflour
3oz (75g) low-fat curd cheese
2oz (50g) Cheddar cheese, grated

(A few prawns and mussels would be luxury additions to this dish – you don't need many and they do give it panache!)

Poach the fish in a little water. (Keep the liquid for fish stock.) Drain and flake the fish, removing the skin and bones. Heat a little oil in a pan and soften the onion in it gently. Stir in the lemon juice and rind, chicken stock, mustard, pepper and flaked fish. Cook the noodles. Combine the cornflour with the curd cheese and stir this into the mixture until it simmers and thickens. Remove from the heat and stir in the grated cheese. Drain the noodles, place on a heated serving dish, pour over the sauce and serve.

Oily fish

These include whitebait, sardines, sprats, herring,
mackerel and the more expensive salmon and trout.
They're called oily because they contain 5–15% oil, but
it's the more healthy, polyunsaturated kind.

Whitebait are best from February to July. Eat them
whole, grilled, or dusted with flour and fried until crisp.
Serve with brown bread and lemon wedges.

Sprats and *Sardines* are usually cheaper than whitebait
and need gutting before you can cook them. Sprats are
at their best from October to March and sardines from
February to July. They can be baked, grilled or fried.

Herring used to be plentiful but alas no more. We have
over-fished our seas and are now paying the price. The
best season is from July to February.

Mackerel must be eaten really fresh and is available all
year round. Both herring and mackerel can be grilled or
cooked in a parcel with any combination of flavourings
that takes your fancy – lemon, parsley, mustard or
spices are all good. Sharp sauces like gooseberry, apple
or mustard go well with both these fish.

Herrings with apple stuffing   *Serves 4*

---

4 large herrings, gutted and cleaned
Black pepper, freshly ground
8oz (225g) eating apples, cored and grated
1 small onion, diced
2oz (50g) breadcrumbs
Oatmeal

Open out the herrings and season lightly with black
pepper. Combine the apples, onion and breadcrumbs
and spread the mixture evenly over the fish. Fold over
the fish with the stuffing inside and place in a lightly
oiled dish. Sprinkled with oatmeal. Bake at gas mark 4,
350°F (180°C) for 25 minutes.

Baked mackerel and gooseberry sauce

The best way to cook mackerel is also the easiest: just wrap them loosely in kitchen foil with a handful of herbs and a splash of white wine or lemon juice. Bake in a moderately hot oven – gas mark 4, 350°F (180°C) – for 20–30 minutes then remove and serve with gooseberry sauce. Mackerel is a rich fish so I like to serve plain boiled potatoes and a little salad with it.

Gooseberry sauce

If you've a freezer it's worth buying up a few pounds of gooseberries and freezing them away for year-round use. For the sauce stew 8oz (225g) gooseberries (topped and tailed) in a very little water. When soft, beat well, then liquidise or sieve. Stir in 1oz (25g) butter and a teaspoon of sugar if the fruit is very sour. Good also with herrings.

Smoked fish

Smoked trout and smoked mackerel are both excellent to eat as they are or as a principal ingredient for fish pâté. Buy them whole, skin and fillet them and serve with lemon wedges, black pepper and a salad.

Kippers, bloaters and smoked haddock need to be cooked. I don't like the dyed varieties though these are cheaper. A real 'best buy' is smoked cod's roe – try the next recipe for a touch of real luxury.

Taramasalata   *Serves 4*

I don't know why this is expensive to buy ready-made because the ingredients are so cheap. Although you can mash everything up using a pestle and mortar the whole thing is simplicity itself if you have a liquidiser. It is perfect for parties as a spread or dip, as a first course with pitta bread, or as part of a main salad platter for warm summer evenings.

I can (3½oz/100g) smoked cod roe
4oz (110g) fresh white breadcrumbs
2–4fl oz (50–100ml) olive oil (home-made, see p.130)
Juice of 1 large lemon
A squirt of garlic purée
Black pepper, freshly ground

Soak the bread in water for a few minutes then squeeze dry. Put in a liquidiser with the garlic purée, lemon juice and 1fl oz (25ml) of the oil. Blend until smooth, then a little at a time, slowly add the cod's roe and remaining oil alternately. (The more oil you add, the more you end up with, as with mayonnaise.) Blend until the mixture is smooth. Season to taste with black pepper and refrigerate until ready to eat.

Canned fish

No seasons, of course, for this and a real store-cupboard 'must'. I'm never without sardines, pilchards, mackerel and tuna. With those in store, you can rustle up a meal at any time.

Mediterranean tuna risotto   *Serves 4*

8oz (225g) long grain rice
1 large can (7oz/200g) tuna fish, drained and flaked
1 can (10.5oz/300g) condensed mushroom soup
4oz (110g) peas or left-over vegetables
Black pepper, freshly ground

Boil the rice for 5 minutes, then drain, rinse under running water and return to the pan. Stir in the flaked tuna fish and the soup. (Do not add water to the soup.) Add the peas or other vegetables. Bring the mixture to the boil and simmer until all the liquid has been absorbed (about 10 minutes). Season and serve with a salad.

Fried sardines

Tinned sardines and pilchards are remarkably high in food value and cheap with it. In my family, we normally eat our sardines drained and mashed with a little vinegar or lemon juice in brown bread sarnies. They fill a gap but they deserve better. This very original way of cooking tinned sardines makes a tasty meal for one person or an unusual starter for the grand dinner party. Buy a good brand as they will be larger and easier to handle – cheap ones are often broken.

Tinned sardines in oil
Seasoned wholewheat flour
Brown bread and butter
Lemon wedges
Black pepper, freshly ground

Drain the sardines well but keep the oil. Rinse the fish under the cold tap to get rid of excess oil and drain on kitchen paper. Toss in seasoned flour. Heat the sardine oil in a small frying pan and gently put in the sardines. Reduce heat slightly and fry the fish until the coating is crisp and golden. Drain on kitchen paper and serve hot with brown bread and butter and a wedge of lemon. Hand round the pepper mill.

MEAT

For true economy the best place to buy fresh meat is at the local butcher. However tempting the displays of pre-wrapped meat are in supermarkets, you miss out on the advice, bones and bargains that you get from your neighbourhood shop. If you respect your butcher he will come to respect you and make sure that you get value for money. He can tell you about seasonal prices – for example, English lamb becomes affordable some time in July and as a result, the price of New Zealand lamb often falls as well. He'll cut you exactly the amount you want, no more and no less, and won't mind a bit if you only want enough for one. I buy my bacon from the butcher too because he cuts his own. This means that I can often buy bacon scraps for adding to risottos and pasta dishes. Some good supermarkets also sell bacon scraps – well worth looking out for.

Poultry and rabbit

The good news is that we can buy rabbit and poultry much more cheaply than red meat, *and* they're better for us. Chicken and turkey should always be bought fresh if possible for the best flavour. Although you can often get a bargain with the frozen variety, don't forget that you're also paying for quite a lot of frozen water.

☆ *Never buy chicken portions. It's always cheaper to buy the whole bird and portion it up yourself. One chicken makes 8 good portions – see p.42 for 'how-to-do-it' diagrams.*

At least 8oz (225g) of the weight of an average bird is in its bones, so it's worth paying a little more for a plumper bird. But the bones are valuable too for the chicken stock. Pressure cooking is an excellent way of cooking a whole chicken and a great time-saver when it comes to making chicken stock from the carcass.

Chicken stock

Chicken carcass and giblets
1 onion, chopped
1 carrot, chopped
Bay leaf

Put the carcass (break this up into small pieces to extract all the flavour) and any skin and giblets in a pan. Cover with water. Add the onion, carrot and bay leaf. Simmer for at least 1 hour, or, if using a pressure cooker, cook at high pressure for 30 minutes, then reduce pressure immediately with cold water. Cool and strain off the liquid. Carefully remove the meat from the bones – there'll be quite a useful amount to use in pies, pasties and savoury pancakes. Refrigerate the stock overnight and remove the fat. Reboil the stock until the volume has reduced by one third.

Cool and either pour into ice cube trays or let it set to a jelly which can be cut into chunks and frozen. The blocks of concentrated stock can be used in many recipes – just add their weight in water to make up to the required amount.

☆ *If you're left with a carcass and you haven't time to make stock that day, then put the whole lot in a poly bag and pop in the freezer. Collect up one or two carcasses and make one big batch.*

Chicken and barley soup   Serves 4

A dish that uses up all the 'unusable' bits of a chicken. Wings, neck, giblets can all go in this soup. Even the pearl barley can be the 'left-overs' from making lemon barley water (see p.125). One of the cheapest and most nourishing soups around.

1lb (450g) chicken bits (more if possible)
1 pint (570ml) chicken stock
2 carrots, diced
1 potato, diced
1 celery stump and leaves, chopped
2 onions, chopped
Black pepper, freshly ground
3–4oz (75–110g) pearl barley (cooked or uncooked)
A few mushrooms stalks
Plenty of chopped fresh herbs, e.g. parsley, tarragon

Put the chicken pieces in large pan with the stock. Bring to the boil and skim off the foam. Add the vegetables and seasoning. Partially cover the pan and simmer for 30 minutes. Add the barley and mushroom stalks and simmer on for a further hour. (If using pre-cooked barley reduce the time to 30 minutes.) Remove the chicken pieces and throw away the skin, gristle and bones. Return any flesh and the liver, finely chopped, to the pan. Stir in herbs and serve.

Note: You can add extra protein by adding some chopped lean ham 30 minutes before serving.

Succotash   *Serves 4*

1 onion, chopped
Cooking oil
1½lb (700g) potatoes, cooked in their skins, cooled and diced
8oz (225g) cooked turkey or chicken, cut into chunks
4oz (110g) good quality sausages, cooked
1 small can (7.94oz/225g) baked beans
1 small can (7oz/198g) whole kernel corn

Fry the onion in a little oil until golden brown. Add the remaining ingredients including the liquid from the cans and cook over a medium heat for about 10–12 minutes. Serve with a green vegetable.

Jointing a Chicken

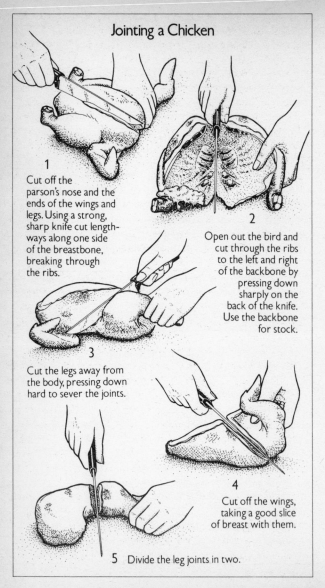

1
Cut off the parson's nose and the ends of the wings and legs. Using a strong, sharp knife cut lengthways along one side of the breastbone, breaking through the ribs.

2
Open out the bird and cut through the ribs to the left and right of the backbone by pressing down sharply on the back of the knife. Use the backbone for stock.

3
Cut the legs away from the body, pressing down hard to sever the joints.

4
Cut off the wings, taking a good slice of breast with them.

5 Divide the leg joints in two.

Chicken 'n' cheese pancakes

Serves 4

It's always worth making up a pile of pancakes in advance and freezing them away between sheets of greaseproof paper (for recipe see p.117). Try mixing different flours for a nuttier, more satisfying pancake. For instance, try half plain flour and half buckwheat or wholewheat – you'll be impressed with the result.

---

8 ready-made thin pancakes

Filling:
2oz (50g) butter
2oz (50g) flour
1 teaspoon dry mustard
1 pint (570ml) skimmed milk
4oz (110g) Cheddar cheese, grated
1 onion, finely chopped and fried
8–12oz (225–350g) cooked chicken, finely chopped
2 tablespoons tomato 'pizza' sauce (see p.129)

To make the filling put the butter, flour, mustard and milk into a saucepan and heat, stirring all the time until the mixture boils and thickens. Add 3oz (75g) of the cheese. Transfer about a third of the sauce into a jug. Stir the fried onion and chopped chicken into the rest of the sauce. Spread each pancake thinly with tomato sauce. Divide the chicken filling between the pancakes and roll them up. Arrange in a shallow baking dish and pour over the reserved sauce. Top with the remaining cheese and bake at gas mark 5, 375°F (190°C) for 30 minutes or until the cheese is golden brown. Serve with a salad.

Romany pot

Serves 4

Sadly today most of us have to buy many of the ingredients which in the past – if you were in the right place at the right time – were free for the taking. Nevertheless this dish is still very economical. I originally demonstrated it on the BBC programme *Pebble Mill at One* a couple of years ago as part of a three-course meal for four people where I had been allowed to spend no more than £1.50 *total*. Having worked out the starter and the pudding, the remaining money (98p) went on this dish.

Cooking oil
1 large onion, roughly chopped
8oz (225g) frozen diced rabbit, thawed and tossed in flour
Left-over chicken scraps from a carcass, tossed in flour
Few mushrooms stalks
1 tablespoon bramble jelly
1 tablespoon red wine concentrate (optional)
2oz (50g) wholewheat flour
Sprig of thyme
1½lb (700g) mixed root vegetables scrubbed clean and coarsley chopped: carrot, baby turnip, potato etc.
Black pepper, freshly ground
4 tablespoons sage and onion stuffing mix
1 egg yolk

Heat the oil in a pan and fry the onion until transparent. Drain and place the onion in the bottom of a casserole. Adding a little more oil to the pan, lightly fry the floured rabbit and chicken. Drain and add to the casserole with the mushroom stalks. To the pan add the bramble jelly, 15fl oz (400ml) water and the wine concentrate, if using, and bring to the boil. Pour over the meat in the casserole, adding the sprig of thyme and the prepared vegetables. Season to taste.

Mix the stuffing with the egg yolk and a little water if necessary, form into balls and add to the casserole. Cover and cook at gas mark 2, 300°F (150°C) for 1 hour or until the vegetables are soft.

Turkey burgers

A good way to use up left-over turkey. Uncooked burgers can be frozen for up to three months.

☆ *Running costs for freezers are high. To make sure you get the best value, try to keep your freezer full. If necessary, fill up the extra space with ice cubes.*

8oz (225g) cooked turkey, finely chopped
4oz (110g) dried breadcrumbs
1 small onion, grated
Black pepper, freshly ground
1 egg
1 tablespoon cooking oil

In a bowl mix all the ingredients except the oil together with 2 tablespoons of water. Shape into 4 flat round burgers. Heat the oil in a pan and fry the burgers for about 10 minutes, turning once.

Serve in sesame seed buns or wholemeal baps with a salad.

Ploughman's pot

12oz (350g) white cabbage
2oz (50g) bacon scraps
1 onion, chopped
1 dessertspoon wholewheat flour
1 tablespoon tomato purée
10fl oz (300ml) turkey stock (made from bones)
Black pepper, freshly ground
1 large apple, cored and sliced
6oz (175g) cooked turkey, diced
4oz (110g) good quality sausages, cooked
Fresh parsley, chopped

Finely shred the cabbage and cook in boiling water for
five minutes. Drain well (but keep the water). Gently fry
the bacon until the fat begins to flow, add the onion and
fry both for about 3 minutes. Stir in the flour and cook
for 1 minute. Add the tomato purée and stock, stir until
thickened, adding the cabbage water if the mixture
seems too thick. Season to taste.

Layer the cabbage, apple, meat and sliced sausages
in a casserole. Cover with the sauce and cook for 1 hour
at gas mark 4, 350°F (180°C). Stir well, sprinkle with
chopped parsley and serve hot with jacket potatoes.

Somerset casserole   *Serves 4*
Whether this is made with rabbit on the bone or frozen
rabbit cubes depends a lot on the price. As there is a
lot of bone in proportion to meat this is where you'll
begin to see the advantages of costing things out first.

8oz (225g) dried prunes
Orange juice
2⅓lb (1kg 125g) rabbit on the bone, or 1½lb (700g)
boned cubed rabbit
1 large onion, chopped
5fl oz (150ml) cider
Bay leaf
10fl oz (300ml) chicken stock
1 tablespoon redcurrant jelly
Black pepper, freshly ground
1oz (25g) cornflour
2 tablespoons malt vinegar
Fresh parsley, chopped

In one bowl combine the prunes and enough orange
juice to cover them. In another bowl combine the
rabbit, onion, cider and bay leaf. Leave both overnight in
the fridge.

Place the rabbit and its marinade in a saucepan or
casserole with the stock and redcurrant jelly. Season

with pepper and bring to the boil. Drain the prunes and add to the casserole. Cover and cook for $1\frac{1}{2}$ hours or until the rabbit is tender. Drain the liquid into another pan, blend the cornflour with the vinegar and stir this into the liquid. Bring to the boil to thicken and simmer for 3 minutes, stirring all the time. Pour the sauce over the rabbit, sprinkle with chopped parsley and serve.

Beef, lamb and pork

This is the one section of our housekeeping bill which is easy to cut down. If you look at the diagrams for beef, lamb and pork, you'll see that there are plenty of economical cuts from which to choose. Generally speaking, all the tender meat is towards the rear end. The main advantage of these cuts is that they cook more quickly, but the food value is the same for any *lean* stewing meat as for the best fillet.

So remember – protein value doesn't change with the cut, although you have to make allowances for any visible fat. We don't need this fat and it's always better to buy meat in a whole piece and trim, cut and mince it at home. This way you'll get better value for money.

Because things like pulses, oatmeal and barley are cheaper sources of protein, it's worth hunting out meat recipes where these are included, so that you can then use less meat. With practice you'll discover that you can use less and less meat and more and more of the vegetable protein and *still* end up with a meaty flavour.

All the cheaper meats need long, slow cooking otherwise they'll be tough. You can't hurry things up. On the other hand they can cook quite happily all day long on the lowest heat which releases you from having to keep an eye on them. Slow cookers are perfect for this as they use hardly any fuel, and do a remarkable job on tenderising cheaper cuts of meat. Pressure cooking, while admittedly speeding up the process, doesn't produce the wonderful flavour that you can achieve by cooking with the slow method.

Cuts of Meat

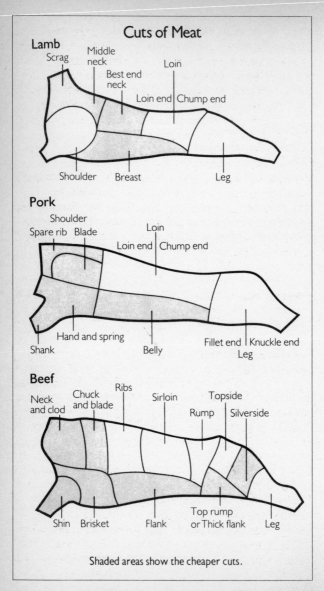

Lamb
- Scrag
- Middle neck
- Best end neck
- Loin
- Loin end
- Chump end
- Shoulder
- Breast
- Leg

Pork
- Shoulder
- Spare rib
- Blade
- Loin
- Loin end
- Chump end
- Hand and spring
- Shank
- Belly
- Fillet end
- Knuckle end
- Leg

Beef
- Neck and clod
- Chuck and blade
- Ribs
- Sirloin
- Topside
- Rump
- Silverside
- Shin
- Brisket
- Flank
- Top rump or Thick flank
- Leg

Shaded areas show the cheaper cuts.

Beef stock

The best time to shop for bones is usually on Monday or Tuesday when the local butcher joints up his beef for the week. Fresh sheet ribs make wonderful stock and if you're a regular customer you'll probably get all bones for free. If not they won't cost more than a few pence.

Prepared in exactly the same way as for chicken stock, I also include the brown onion skins as they darken the stock. But even though, like chicken stock, beef bones can also be cooked by pressure I prefer to do them as slowly as possible in my slow cooker because this results in a much richer flavour. You should never be in hurry with beef. Any meat left on the bones will drop off and can be used in the same way as chicken scraps. If you don't use too much water initially you won't need to reduce the stock further and it will set into a firm jelly.

Onion soup   *Serves 4*

1 large onion, very finely sliced
Cooking oil
1 dessertspoon flour
1½ pints (900ml) beef stock
Black pepper, freshly ground
1 slice of French bread per person, about 1 in (2.5cm) thick
Grated cheese

Fry the onion gently in the oil, stirring all the time, until the slices are soft. Sprinkle with flour and stir until pale gold. Add the stock – a little at a time – and keep stirring until it boils. Then lower the heat and simmer for 10 minutes. Season to taste.

Sprinkle the grated cheese on the slices of bread and pop them under a grill to toast. Pour the soup into a tureen or individual dishes and float the toast on top.

Poor man's jugged hare

Serves 4

This is a very old recipe, full of flavour and nothing to do with hares at all. Any gravy left over could be added to beef stock to make tomorrow's *Soupe du Jour*.

1lb (450g) lean shin beef, cubed
Flour
Cooking oil
6 cloves
1 onion, peeled
1 lemon
1 teaspoon mixed dried herbs
Black pepper, freshly ground
1 packet (3oz/85g) parsley and thyme stuffing mix
1 egg yolk
2 sticks celery, finely grated
Cornflour
1 dessertspoon tomato purée

Toss the beef in the flour and lightly fry in a little oil. Drain and place in a casserole with the whole onion which has been studded with the cloves. Grate half the lemon rind and peel the remaining rind being careful not to include the pith. Cut this rind into strips. Add the strips, herbs and a few grinds of pepper to the meat mixture, adding a very little water. Cover tightly and cook at gas mark 2, 300°F (150°C) until the meat is tender – about 3 hours (5–6 hours in a slow cooker).

Make the stuffing as directed on the packet, adding the grated lemon rind and juice, egg yolk and celery. Form this into balls and bake in an oiled tin on the shelf above the meat for 30 minutes, or, if using a slow cooker, add to the casserole at the beginning of cooking.

When the beef is cooked, strain off the gravy and thicken this with cornflour paste. Stir in the tomato purée, adding more water or beef stock if necessary.

Serve the meat on a dish with the gravy poured over, surrounded with stuffing balls. Offer a dish of redcurrant jelly to go with it.

Poitrine d'agneau au chou

Serves 4

This is offered to you under its French title because if I said 'Breast of Lamb with Cabbage' you wouldn't want to know. But it's such a tasty recipe, making the most of the least interesting meat imaginable. We always used to eat breast of lamb rolled and stuffed and I hated it. This is quite different.

---

1 small white cabbage, finely shredded
1 large onion, finely chopped
2oz (50g) bacon scraps
Cooking oil
4oz (110g) porridge oats
Grated rind and juice of 1 lemon
1 breast of lamb
Black pepper, freshly ground
Fresh parsley, chopped

Cook the cabbage for 5 minutes in a little water and drain well. Fry the onion and bacon scraps in a little oil. Mix together the cabbage, bacon, onion, oats, lemon rind and juice and arrange in an oiled heatproof dish. Cut the lamb into ribs and place on top of the cabbage mixture skin side up. Season with pepper and cook at gas mark 6, 400°F (200°C) for about 1 hour until the meat is tender. Sprinkle with parsley and serve with rice or jacket potatoes and a salad.

☆ *Try this economical sauce for fish, meat or salads: liquidise outer leaves and stalks of e.g. lettuce, cabbage, parsley, watercress and celery stumps with natural yoghurt and freshly ground black pepper.*

Lamb and lentil casserole

10fl oz (300ml) beef stock
4oz (110g) green lentils
1 onion, chopped
2 carrots, sliced
1 small potato per person, sliced
12oz (350g) lean lamb, cubed
Redcurrant jelly
Black pepper, freshly ground
Fresh parsley, chopped

Bring the stock to the boil. Put the lentils in a casserole and pour in the stock. Add the vegetables. Stir in the cubed lamb, season, cover and cook at gas mark 4, 350°F (180°C) for about 1½ hours or until the meat and vegetables are tender.

About 15 minutes before the end of the cooking time remove the lid and stir in the redcurrant jelly. Add a little water if the casserole seems dry. Replace the lid and continue cooking until done. Sprinkle with chopped parsley, and serve.

Note: If you want to use less meat, substitute extra lentils and vegetables.

Barbecued spare ribs

Serves 4

This recipe uses barbecue sauce which I find is an extremely useful sauce to keep in the store cupboard. You can use it with any kind of meat for cooking and, if you dilute it with more vinegar, you can also use it as a marinade.

A marinade is an acid-based liquid (lemon juice, vinegar or wine) in which you soak meat for several hours. This helps to tenderise it and is very good for stir-frying, kebabs and anything barbecued.

1lb (450g) piece of pork spare rib

For the sauce:
2 tablespoons soy sauce
2 tablespoons honey
2 tablespoons plum jam
1 tablespoon vinegar
1 teaspoon Worcestershire sauce
1 teaspoon dry mustard
2 tablespoons tomato purée or ketchup

Blend all the sauce ingredients in a pan over a low heat and bring to the boil. (Note: This can be transferred to a hot sterilised jar, sealed with cling-film and a screwcap lid and kept in store until needed.)

Pre-heat the oven to gas mark 6, 400°F (200°C). Cut the piece of pork spare rib into separate ribs and bake in the oven for about 10 minutes. Drain away the fat and coat the ribs on both sides with barbecue sauce. Bake for a further 10–15 minutes basting with the sauce until it has thickened and the ribs are crispy. Eat hot with the fingers as a starter or with rice as part of a main meal.

Stretching meat a little further

Two ways of serving an attractive plateful without going to town on the meat are kebabs and stir-fry dishes.

Kebabs Cut the meat into cubes (I prefer lean pork or lamb) and marinate (see opposite). Thread alternate pieces of meat, onion, pepper, bay leaf, small tomato and mushroom on skewers, brush with oil and cook under a hot grill or on a barbecue. Served with plenty of rice and an inexpensive salad such as coleslaw, no-one will notice they haven't had their 'pound of flesh'!

☆ *Look out for flat skewers. They prevent the goodies rolling back every time you turn them.*

Stir-fry This is one of the best ways I know of making a little go a long, long way. The secret of successful stir-frying is first the chopping and secondly the flavouring.

Meat (beef, lamb, pork or chicken) should be sliced into thin slices or slivers across the grain of the flesh. Don't use a really cheap cut for stir-frying. It's far better to buy a smaller amount of a better-quality meat, although you can improve the tenderness of, for example, shoulder pork by marinating it (see p.52).

Chop your vegetables into small even-sized pieces. Long thin vegetables such as carrots should be cut on the diagonal (see illustration) so that a large surface area is exposed to the heat.

As far as flavourings are concerned, garlic, fresh root ginger and spring onions are essential for a truly authentic taste. I buy fresh ginger in small amounts from the greengrocer. It's not something I eat everyday so I ask for a small 2 inch (5cm) section. Peel and grate just as much as you need. Crush or finely chop fresh garlic and slice spring onions thinly on the diagonal.

Prepare all your ingredients first, then heat a little oil (I use sunflower) in a large heavy frying-pan or a wok if you've got one. Put in the three aromatic flavourings first, then the meat and harder vegetables (e.g. cauliflower), and finally any softer ingredients such as mushrooms. A dash of soy sauce doesn't come amiss either. Keep stirring and shaking the pan to make sure the ingredients don't burn. Above all, don't overcook a stir-fry dish – it's supposed to taste light and *crunchy*.

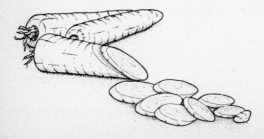

Liver

There are various kinds of liver – the larger the beast, the coarser the liver and the stronger the flavour. Pig's liver is best for all-round purposes. Lamb's liver is more expensive and chicken livers have the mildest flavour.

Liver dumplings

Makes 12–16 dumplings

Meat or vegetable stock
4oz (110g) pig's liver, finely chopped
1 egg, beaten
Grated rind of ½ orange
1 onion, finely grated
1 dessertspoon fresh parsley, finely chopped
3oz (75g) wholewheat breadcrumbs (if the mixture turns out too soft, add a little more)
Nutmeg, freshly grated
Black pepper, freshly ground

Heat the stock to boiling point in a saucepan. Meanwhile mix all the other ingredients in a bowl. Shape into balls about the size of a walnut and drop into the boiling stock. Cover and reduce the heat to a simmer. Cook for about 7 minutes. Drain and serve hot with a savoury sauce, and noodles or rice.

Savoury sauce

This is a versatile sauce-cum-gravy which you can alter according to the dish you're eating.

1 onion, chopped
Cooking oil
½oz (10g) flour
10fl oz (300ml) concentrated beef stock, home-made
Black pepper, freshly ground

Fry the onion gently in the oil. Stir in the flour and continue to cook gently for 1 minute. Slowly add the beef stock and stir until it thickens. Season to taste.

You can add a squirt of garlic purée to the onion if you fancy it. Or hot up the sauce with a dash of brown sauce, Worcestershire sauce or even Tabasco. Or keep it subtle by stirring in a few herbs and a little yoghurt. The juice from a can of tomatoes and a pinch of basil and/or marjoram gives it another dimension.

The variable stroganoff   *Serves 4*

Traditionally made with best beef, this is one way to make a piece of meat go a long way. And it's even cheaper if you choose to make it with chicken or liver. Yoghurt substitutes beautifully for sour cream and with all this money saving you can afford to include the sherry.

12oz (350g) pig's liver, or chicken, or chicken livers, cut into thin strips
Cooking oil
1 large onion, chopped
1 tablespoon flour
10fl oz (300ml) chicken stock
1 teaspoon paprika
4oz (50g) mushrooms, sliced
Black pepper, freshly ground
1 dessertspoon cooking sherry

To serve:
8oz (100g) long-grain rice
Natural yoghurt

Fry the strips of meat in a little hot oil until sealed on all sides. Remove from the pan with a slotted spoon and set aside. Add the onion to the juices in the pan and fry until it turns transparent. Then stir in the flour, and gradually add the chicken stock, stirring all the time, until the mixture thickens. Add the paprika, mushrooms, pepper and the meat and simmer for 20 minutes, stirring in the sherry near the end. Cook the rice while the stroganoff is simmering.

Make a bed of hot rice on a plate and top with the stroganoff. Swirl over yoghurt and serve with a dish of green vegetables.

My house pâté

4oz (110g) pig's liver
½ onion, chopped
1oz (25g) bacon scraps
1 teaspoon wine concentrate
Black pepper, freshly ground
1 egg yolk (optional)
2oz (50g) unsalted butter, softened

Put all the ingredients except the butter into a liquidiser and whizz to a pulp. (Alternatively, put through a mincer.) Spread the mixture in an oiled loaf tin and cover with butter paper. Stand the tin in a roasting tin half full of hot water and bake at gas 3, 325°F (170°C) for 1 hour. Remove the pâté from the tin and put through a vegetable mill or sieve to remove any stringy bits. Cool slightly and work in the butter. Add more pepper if needed. Pot up and chill. This pâté freezes well.

4
VEGETABLES AND FRUIT

I'm always pleased when I discover that looking for ways of making things go further has more than penny-pinching behind it. Nutritionists would like us to eat more of our vegetables and fruit unpeeled and uncooked for health reasons. And, of course, taking their advice, we save on fuel costs. So cheapest is best!

But don't always try to *buy* the cheapest. It really is important to buy top quality produce because it avoids wastage and there's less vitamin deterioration. Sometimes it's worth paying a penny or two more just to make sure because vitamins and minerals are very important to us – when we don't take in enough our bodies can't function properly.

Unlike carbohydrates, fats and proteins, vitamins have a very short life. Up to 25% of vitamins may be destroyed an hour after picking a crop. Some dissolve in water and others can easily be destroyed by heat. Quite a lot more just get thrown away because most of the nutrients are concentrated close to the skin or in the darker (outer) leaves of greenstuff.

My advice is to peel and cook only if absolutely necessary, and when you *do* cook, to use as little water as possible (steaming is even better). Any trimmings and cooking water can be used for soups. Just make sure you wash your fruit and vegetables well before eating the skins – you never know what chemicals they may have been sprayed with these days. Keep in mind that nature has done a remarkable little package deal when it comes to fruit and vegetables, giving us exceptional food value for low cost *so long as we interfere with the produce as little as possible before we eat it.*

In other words, Pandora, don't open the box!

Shopping

I try to avoid buying those plastic bags of pre-packed vegetables. They usually cost more per pound than loose ones. If you buy where things are sold loose, you can make your own selection. But don't buy too much at a time – fresh foods should never be stored longer than necessary – and shop around.

Supermarkets have such high standards that even when they reduce prices to clear stock you can be sure that the quality is high. But these standards can sometimes mean that you could be paying more per pound than in a local greengrocer's. The local shop may not have so much variety but you could make a big saving on seasonal produce. Compare prices before buying.

Storing

All vegetables need to be kept cool if you want them to keep their goodness. The firm vegetables – cabbage, root crops etc – are best stored where air can circulate. Keep softer salad vegetables in the bottom drawer of the refrigerator.

Growing your own

Of course, the freshest possible produce is that which you've grown yourself, but we haven't all got the time or the space to go back to the land. You may, though, have one apple tree or one plum tree which every so often goes mad and inundates you with fruit. When this happens, my squirrel-like instincts come to the fore and the cupboards and freezer fill up with preserves and purées ready for the winter. It's exhausting, though, and I sometimes wish nature regulated things a bit better.

But one thing I always do is grow my own herbs. All you need is a sunny windowsill and you'll find your cooking leaps into another class when you add fresh home-grown herbs. I've also discovered another treat –

I grow my own peppers and aubergines on the windowsill too. These aren't cheap to buy because imported produce is liable to deteriorate in transit from the country of origin and the greengrocer has to cover the cost of wastage. If you can grow half a dozen plants of each, the crop may well see you through until the next season, if you're lucky.

I freeze any surplus peppers. All you need to do is wash and dry them and remove the stalks. Cut them in half, remove the seeds, then either cut them in slices or dice. There's no need to blanch. Just freeze in bags and crunch them up before they are fully frozen to keep them 'free-flow'. Red peppers have twice the vitamin C content of green ones, so if you're growing your own, leave them on the plant till they turn red.

Don't forget mustard and cress – they're so easy to grow on the windowsill. And my other crop which I wouldn't be without doesn't even need a sunny windowsill. I have a permanent container of sprouting seeds on the go, ready to pop into a daily salad. The easiest and cheapest way of sprouting seeds is the jar method. All you need is glass jar (an orange juice jar, large coffee jar or bottling jar is best), piece of muslin or nylon stocking and a rubber band. You don't need expensive 'sprouting kits' or any other special equipment. This is what you do:

1 Soak 1 dessertspoon of the seeds in tepid water overnight.
2 Put the seeds in the jar and secure the muslin over the top with the rubber band.
3 Fill the jar three quarters full with tepid or cold water, shake the jar to rinse the seeds, then drain off the water through the muslin top.
4 Put the jar on its side in a warm, dark but airy place.
5 Rinse the seeds every morning and evening with water and drain them as just described.

The seeds will take between 4 and 6 days to grow, depending on the type of seed and the growing

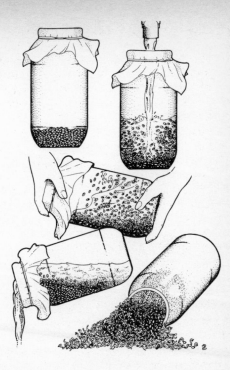

conditions. The main thing which can go wrong is that the seeds will start to smell musty – this could be because you're keeping them in too hot a place or rinsing them with too hot water. Step up the rinsing if you think they're beginning to smell odd. It's up to seven times cheaper to grow your own beansprouts than to buy a pack already sprouted. Store the sprouts in a bowl of water in the fridge and change the water every day.

Perhaps my greatest triumph has been a box of mushrooms – my last crop gave me just over 4lb (1.8kg) at less than half the cost of shop-bought ones.

So away with the spider plants and busy lizzies and in with the herbs, peppers and aubergines. Clear a space for the sprouts and mushrooms and you're quids in. A classy ratatouille becomes an everyday dish.

Ratatouille

4 tablespoons cooking oil
2 medium onions, sliced
1 green pepper, de-seeded and sliced
2 aubergines, sliced
1 courgette, sliced
3 tomatoes, skinned and sliced
Salt
Black pepper, freshly ground
A squirt of garlic purée

Heat the oil in a flameproof casserole and stir in all the ingredients. Turn the vegetables in the hot oil for about 2 minutes, then cover and cook for $1\frac{1}{4}$ hours in the oven at gas mark 4, 350°F (180°C).

Exotics

Over the last few years, the range of fruit and vegetables available in the shops has increased enormously. Things we only knew about from reading of travels in faraway lands are now commonplace in the local greengrocer's. But because they're imported, they're naturally expensive. I never like to be deprived of a new taste experience so it dawned on me that just like our own produce, these foreigners must have their seasons. There must be a time when the price comes down a bit.

Here is a selection which shows when the prices should be at their lowest.

Aubergines Supplies are available all year round from countries both sides of the equator, but best value is usually found *between January and April*. Remember though – it's easy to grow your own.

Avocados An all year round fruit but the price often comes down *just before Christmas*.

Apricots The best supplies are from Spain, France and Italy *in June and July*.

Cherries *From June to August* is best with supplies from England, Italy, Spain and France.

Grapes Small, seedless green grapes are cheaper *in July and August* but you can also find good bargains in the larger grapes all year round.

Kiwifruit Our main supply comes from New Zealand *from June to January*. One kiwifruit goes a long way thinly sliced.

Limes Available all year round.

Melons Best value in honeydew melons is in the months of *June, August, September and October*.

☆ *Melon shells make excellent containers for serving dips or ice cream or fruit salad. Take out the flesh with a scoop, cut a piece off the bottom to make a flat base and put in the freezer until needed.*

Pineapples Supplies come mainly from African countries with best value *from October to May*.

☆ *Grow your pineapple tops as plants – an exotic gift.*

Peaches and Nectarines Best value is in *July and August*. These rarely need peeling.

The aim of this book is not to encourage buying only the cheapest, but to *begin* with the cheapest so that you will be able to afford everything you need … *and more*. This way you can have your cake (or kiwifruit) – and eat it too.

VEGETABLES

Raw vegetables

Just about any vegetable (except perhaps potatoes) can be eaten raw all year round. It not only saves on fuel but it's also the best way to eke out just a few vegetables because anything grated or shredded always looks a lot more. It even takes longer to eat. However, exposure to the air is not good for cut surfaces of vegetables so aim to prepare them immediately before serving. If there has to be a delay cover closely with cling-film.

Do experiment with different combinations of vegetables in salads. You can be really creative finding out what combinations of herbs, spices and dressings go best with which ingredients.

Here are some which I enjoy.

Crunchy cauliflower salad   *Serves 4*

---

1 small cauliflower
1 carrot, finely sliced
1 onion, finely chopped
4 tomatoes, skinned and sliced
French dressing

Wash the cauliflower and break it into small florets. In a large bowl, mix all the ingredients together and toss in the dressing.

☆ *You can freeze tomatoes just as they are. When you want to use them, pop them in hot water and the skins slide off.*

Beetroot and orange salad   *Serves 2*

2 raw beetroot, peeled and grated
Grated zest of 1 large orange
5fl oz (150ml) natural yoghurt

Mix all the ingredients together – a very colourful salad.

Seven leaf salad   *Serves 4*

1 small lettuce
As much as you can spare of six fresh herbs (my
favourite selection is borage, mint, lemon balm,
marjoram, sorrel, parsley)
French dressing

Wash the lettuce and herbs, chop roughly and place in a
bowl. Add a little dressing and toss. Leave in a cool
place for an hour for the flavours to develop.

☆ *If you grow your own herbs, don't be afraid to pick*
  them vigorously. The more you pick, the more
  they'll grow and the more you'll get.

Stir-fry vegetables

If you don't want your vegetables raw, the next best
thing is to stir-fry them. Cooked like this, they're
crunchy and flavoursome. You don't need elaborate
Chinese wok arrangements, a large frying pan works just
as well. If you're not an experienced stir-frier, turn to
p.54 for some helpful hints. The most important thing is
to get everything chopped before you start cooking.
Cabbage, cauliflower, turnip, carrot, peppers, Brussels
sprouts, celery, courgettes – the list is endless. Chop the
tougher vegetables into smaller bits and cook them first,
gradually adding the ones that take less time.

Heat a little oil in the pan and, when hot, stir in finely chopped fresh garlic and fresh root ginger and some thinly sliced spring onions. Then, starting with the tougher vegetables, gradually add them all, stirring continuously. The whole thing should only take minutes as the aim is to get the vegetables just softened on the outside but crunchy in the middle. You can add bits of cooked chicken, bacon or fish and serve with rice for a complete meal.

Soup Home-made soups are one of the best value-for-money foods going. You can add almost anything you've got and every time I make some, the mixture is different.

Here's a starter to which you can add your own variations.

Basic lettuce soup ... plus   *Serves 4–6*

---

1 onion, chopped
Cooking oil
Outside leaves and stalks of lettuces (the more you have, the tastier it gets)
1½ pints (900ml) chicken stock
Handful of peas (or pea pods)
Black pepper, freshly ground
Sugar

Fry the onion lightly in a little oil. Shred the lettuce leaves, add them to the pan and fry on for a few minutes. Pour in the chicken stock, peas (or pea pods), season with a little pepper and a pinch of sugar and simmer gently for half an hour. Pour into a liquidiser and whizz to a pulp. Or you can put it through a vegetable mill or sieve.

When you sieve you'll be left with an appreciable amount of vegetable purée. Try spreading it on hot

toast, top with grated cheese and brown under the grill.
If you make this soup in the summer, you can add
sorrel, lemon balm, tarragon, chives, watercress leaves
and stems, or any complementary herb.

Minestrone soup Serves 4–6

You can make this with either beef or chicken stock and
it contains all sorts of goodies. This is as near to the
classical Italian version as I can get but feel free to make
up your own variation.

1½ pints (900ml) beef or chicken stock
2oz (50g) dried haricot beans
2 tablespoons cooking oil
1lb (450g) diced mixed vegetables, e.g. unpeeled
courgettes, carrots, potatoes, celery, cabbage
½ onion, finely chopped
1 small can (8oz/227g) tomatoes, drained and chopped
2 sprigs parsley
1 small bay leaf
2 level tablespoons long-grain rice
2oz (50g) cooked ham, chopped (optional)

Bring the stock to the boil and add the beans. Boil
rapidly for 10 minutes. (This is important as it neutralises
any toxins.) Remove from the heat and leave to stand
for at least an hour. Return to the heat and simmer until
the beans are tender (1–1½ hours). Meanwhile heat the
oil in a pan and add the chopped vegetables. Cook for
2–3 minutes. Stir in the onion. Cook for a further 5
minutes until the vegetables are soft and golden. Stir in
the tomatoes, the stock, beans and herbs. Bring to the
boil and simmer for half an hour. Remove the herbs,
add the rice and ham and cook for a further 15
minutes. Season to taste. Serve hot with a bowl of
grated cheese to garnish.

Note: Instead of rice you can use up broken bits of pasta.

Watercress soup   *Serves 4–6*

1 tablespoon cooking oil
1 large onion, very finely chopped
1 large potato, diced
Big bunch of watercress
1 pint (570ml) chicken stock
Black pepper, freshly ground
10fl oz (300ml) milk

Garnish:
Croutons (small cubes of bread fried until crisp and golden)

Heat the oil in a pan and fry the onion gently for 5 minutes. Add the diced potato and cook on for 5 more minutes. Briefly liquidise the watercress (or chop it finely) with the chicken stock and add this to the onions and potatoes. Season to taste and bring to the boil. Cover and simmer for half an hour. Return the soup to the liquidiser and blend until smooth, or put through a vegetable mill. Pour into a bowl and stir in 10fl oz (300ml) milk. Garnish with croutons. This can be served hot or chilled.

Watercress purée
Blend the leaves and stalks of a big bunch of watercress in a liquidiser until smooth. Mix into a batter for savoury pancakes (see p.103), or use in quiches or in any way you would use spinach purée.

☆ *To keep watercress fresh store head down in a jug of water. Keep chilled and change the water every day.*

6oz (175g) leeks, cleaned and chopped
2 onions, chopped
1 tablespoon cooking oil
1 pint (570ml) chicken stock
Black pepper, freshly ground
1 medium potato, cooked and chopped
Milk

Fry the leeks and onion gently in the oil until pale gold. Pour in the stock and season to taste. Cover and simmer until the vegetables are soft. Add the potato and liquidise or put through a vegetable mill. Return to the pan and re-heat. Stir in a little milk.

Onions

I am *never* without onions. They go into nearly every savoury dish I cook. Eaten raw at the onset of a cold or cough (I couldn't attempt it at any other time) they seem to stop it in its tracks. I don't think the bugs can stand the fumes any more than I can. I prefer to buy the big onions for chopping and slicing and small 'pickling' or shallots to skin and add whole to casseroles. I add the outer skins of onions to beef bones when I'm making stock to give it a lovely golden brown colour.

Celery

This is a 'must' on my shopping list although I don't buy it weekly as it can last a long time.

I pick a sizeable head with plenty of tender green leaves as these can be included in green salads or used to flavour soups and stews. I then work my way down the stick slicing off what I need for casseroles and salads. Even the stump can be grated with the final end included in stock. Celery has such an individual flavour that it's a good substitute for salt in hot dishes.

Potatoes

Aim to buy potatoes loose, choosing small ones of even size for boiling and larger ones for baking. Leave the inbetweens for somebody else. Potatoes are the one vegetable we expect to peel, yet it really isn't necessary. Leaving the skins intact prevents wastage and the potatoes retain all their flavour. Also a lot of the goodness is just under the skin and this is the bit which so often ends up in the bin. Unpeeled potatoes are more satisfying too.

If you do peel potatoes, scrub them well first and remove any bruised bits. Then take off good thick peel for soup, or peel thinly and dry this out in the oven to make your own special crisps.

Pauper's potage

Serves 4–6

1½ pints (900ml) chicken or beef stock
Cooking oil
1 large onion, chopped
Potato peelings from 5 large potatoes, scrubbed
Green tops of 4 leeks, washed and chopped
1 celery stump, grated
1 cabbage stump, grated
Tops and tails of 4 carrots, scrubbed
1 dessertspoon fresh mixed herbs, chopped, or 1 teaspoon dried
1 squirt of garlic purée
Black pepper, freshly ground

Bring the stock to the boil. Meanwhile soften the onion in a little oil over a gentle heat. Stir the onion and the rest of the ingredients into the stock, cover the pan and simmer until the vegetables are soft (about 45 minutes). Put the soup through a vegetable mill, or liquidise, and serve with wholewheat bread.

Note: To make the soup thicker and even more nutritious add 2oz (50g) split lentils in with the vegetables.

☆ *To save 30 minutes' cooking time for jacket potatoes, put the scrubbed potatoes in a bowl and cover with boiling water. Leave to stand for 15–20 minutes. Drain and bake in the oven at gas mark 6, 400°F (200°C) for 30 minutes. If using an electric oven, turn off after 20 minutes and cook on in the cooling oven for a further 15–20 minutes.*

Potato kugel

Serves 4–6

For a really satisfying meatless dish, you'd have to go a long way to beat this one. The amount serves up to six people, but because it can be eaten hot or cold it could make do for a smaller family and carry on being eaten over two days: hot one day, cold the next.

---

6 medium potatoes, grated
3 carrots, grated
1 large onion, finely chopped
2 eggs
2 tablespoons cooking oil
2 tablespoons parsley, chopped
1 slice wholewheat bread, crumbed
2oz (50g) grated cheese
½oz butter or margarine

Combine the potatoes, carrots and onion. Lightly beat the eggs with the oil and pour over the vegetables. Stir in the chopped parsley and breadcrumbs. Spread in a well oiled pie dish, dot with butter or margarine and bake at gas mark 4, 350°F (180°) for about 45 minutes. Sprinkle with the cheese after half an hour. Serve hot with a salad or eat cold with a mug of hot soup.

Carrots

Not only can these be used as vegetables, but they also make very good cakes and puddings.

Carrot cake

This cake, sometimes known as Passion cake, traditionally has a cream cheese icing, but I prefer to use low-fat curd cheese – cheaper and less fatty.

- 4oz (110g) sugar
- 4oz (110g) margarine
- 2 eggs
- 1 dessertspoon black treacle
- ½ teaspoon baking powder
- 6oz (175g) self-raising flour
- 1 teaspoon cinnamon
- 6oz (175g) carrot, finely grated
- 2oz (50g) walnuts, chopped

Icing:
6oz (175g) low-fat curd cheese
2oz (50g) butter
6oz (175g) icing sugar

Grease and flour an 8 inch (20.5cm) ring mould. Beat the sugar and margarine together and add the eggs and treacle. Sift the flour, baking powder and cinnamon. Fold into the mixture. Stir in the carrots and nuts. Bake at gas mark 4, 350°F (180°C) for 1 hour.

To make the icing, beat together the cheese and butter. Add the icing sugar and beat until smooth. Spread over the top of the cooled cake.

☆ *When serving carrots as a vegetable, try baking them in the oven with the main dish. Cut them into sticks and put in an overproof dish with a little oil, herbs and black pepper. Bake covered for 30–40 minutes.*

Carrot and sultana flan   *Serves 4–6*

Worth making on a day when you're going to serve
carrots as you can then plan to cook the extra carrots
you'll be needing for this recipe at the same time. The
egg, sultanas and breadcrumbs all add their own
particular nourishment.

4oz (110g) carrots, cooked
1oz (25g) melted butter
1 beaten egg
1 tablespoon sultanas
2 tablespoons wholewheat breadcrumbs
2 tablespoons caster sugar
Grated rind of 1 lemon
Pinch of grated nutmeg
8oz (225g) shortcrust pastry
Flaked almonds

Sieve the carrots and mix with the butter and egg, or
put the 3 ingredients in a liquidiser and blend to a pulp.
To this mixture add the rest of the ingredients except
the pastry and almonds. Line an 8 inch (20.5cm) pie
plate with the pastry, spread it with the mixture, scatter
a few flaked almonds on top and bake on the top shelf
at gas mark 4, 350°F (180°C) for half an hour.

Turnips

Turnips are, I think, a very underrated vegetable. During
the winter months they are usually very inexpensive.
New baby turnips can be eaten peeled and grated, raw,
in salads. If you are cooking turnips it is worth doing
double to make the following recipe. Pop the assembled
dish in the fridge and then bake it in the oven the next
day along with your main dish or pudding.

Turnips in yoghurt

Serves 4

4 medium turnips, cooked
1 dessertspoon caraway seeds
2–3 tablespoons natural yoghurt
1 dessertspoon fresh basil, chopped, or $\frac{1}{2}$ teaspoon
dried
Black pepper, freshly ground
Juice of 1 lemon

Slice the turnips and place in overlapping layers in an
oiled ovenproof dish. Mix the caraway seeds and basil
with the yoghurt and pour over the turnips. Bake at gas
mark 4, 350°F (180°C) until tender – about 15 minutes.
Season and sprinkle with lemon juice. Serve hot.

Cabbage

Cabbage is sometimes sold by the pound and
sometimes priced individually. Look out for the latter –
you can often find a large cabbage which costs exactly
the same as a smaller one. And, of course, I always buy
the large one! There are often bargains in cabbage in
the late summer and early autumn.

Chop white cabbage finely and make into coleslaw –
and don't forget red cabbage. You can use it in exactly
the same way as white and it gives you a different
flavour and a more colourful dish. For the next recipe,
you can use either white or red cabbage.

Casseroled cabbage

For 4 people finely shred 1lb (450g) cabbage and toss it
together with a teaspoon each of sugar and caraway
seeds. Add a tablespoon of vinegar and 2 cored, sliced
apples. Put in a casserole, cover tightly with a lid or foil
and cook at gas mark 3, 325°F (170°C) for about 1
hour. Cook jacket potatoes at the same time and serve
with cold meat.

Chinese leaves

These have to be worth a mention as they are so good in the winter as an alternative to lettuce which by then is much dearer. I usually work from the top of the 'stick', shredding the tender leaves for salads and using the crispier mid-ribs in stir-fry dishes. The lower end of the stick I cook as cabbage. It's delicious steamed and tossed in butter. One stick, well-wrapped in cling-film and kept in the fridge, sees me through at least one, maybe two, weeks.

Mushrooms

I never peel mushrooms. All they need is a wipe with a damp cloth to remove any bits of compost. I like to use the stalks to make this concentrated mushroom flavouring which I keep in the freezer ready for soups and casseroles.

Mushroom stock cubes

8oz (225g) mushroom stalks
1oz (25g) shallots
1oz (25g) butter

Mince together the mushroom stalks and shallots and fry in the butter till very dry. Pack into ice cube trays to freeze. Store in polythene bags in the freezer for up to 3 months.

☆ *To store mushrooms, line a container with damp kitchen paper and put in the mushrooms. Cover with a little more damp paper and keep in the fridge. They will last up to 1 week or even 2 if they're very fresh.*

Marrows

These are often cheap in the autumn but their size can be daunting. Apart from the well known recipes for baked, stuffed marrows, here are some other ideas you may like to try:

- Grate some marrow and stir it into a batter to fry as savoury fritters.
- Peel and chop some marrow and sauté in a little oil with chopped onion, tomato and some mixed herbs.

Marrow and ginger sorbet   Serves 4

1lb (450g) marrow, peeled, de-seeded and chopped
½oz (10g) preserved ginger, chopped
2oz (50g) granulated sugar
2 level teaspoons powdered gelatine
2 egg whites, stiffly beaten

Poach the marrow in a little water until soft. Drain well, then liquidise with the preserved ginger or put through a vegetable mill. Measure out 15fl oz (400ml) of marrow and ginger purée into a pan and add the sugar and gelatine. Heat gently until the sugar and gelatine have dissolved. Pour into a metal dish, cool and freeze until firm around the edges. Beat sides to middle with a fork to a frozen mush. Fold in the stiffly beaten egg whites, cover and freeze till firm. Thaw slightly before serving. Serve with a slice of melon as a starter.

Vegetable stroganoff   Serves 4

This is a really useful recipe when you've only got small amounts of several vegetables, and although this is a purely vegetarian version of a *stroganoff* you could include a small amount of meat if you wanted. Alternatively, you could add a lot of vegetables to the traditional beef stroganoff to make your meat go further.

4oz mushrooms, chopped
1 large onion, chopped
Cooking oil
1 tablespoon soy sauce
5fl oz (150ml) natural yoghurt
3 tablespoons red wine (optional)
2–3 pint (1.1–1.7 litre) measure of chopped raw
vegetables, e.g. broccoli, cauliflower, carrots, courgettes
8oz (225g) dried spinach noodles
2 tablespoons chopped chives

Fry the mushrooms and onion in the oil until soft, then add the soy sauce and wine. Simmer for a few minutes, stir in the yoghurt and heat through (do not boil). Meanwhile steam the vegetables until tender. Cook the noodles in plenty of boiling water and drain. Spread the noodles in a dish, top with vegetables and cover with the mushroom sauce. Sprinkle with chives.

Vegetable curry
Serves 4

2 onions, chopped
Cooking oil
2 tablespoons curry powder
1 teaspoon malt vinegar
1 dessertspoon tomato purée
1 pint (570ml) stock (meat, chicken or vegetable)
2 pints (1.1 litre) mixed vegetables, coarsely chopped
Flour
Natural yoghurt

Fry the onions in a little oil until they are just turning brown. Stir in the curry powder and fry for 1 minute. Add the vinegar, tomato purée and stock and simmer for 20 minutes. Meanwhile dip the vegetables in flour and fry in oil until light brown. Add them to the curry sauce and cook until tender. Stir in some yoghurt just before serving. Accompany with boiled rice.

☆ *Coriander is a key ingredient in curry powder. The dried seeds are obtainable in supermarkets (spice section), and these can be ground up for curries. If you plant them in the garden or in a pot they will grow and you can have your own fresh coriander leaves (not readily available). Fresh ripe coriander seeds also have their own flavour.*

Aubergines

One fruit (home-grown of course) will feed about two people. The preparation is simple – remove the stem and calyx and cut into slices about $\frac{1}{2}$ inch (1cm) thick. Place on a cloth and sprinkle with salt. After half an hour wipe the salt off the fruit and squeeze dry with a kitchen paper. This draws out the excess water from the fruit.

Aubergines in tomato sauce   *Serves 4*

2 large aubergines, prepared as above
Flour
Cooking oil
1 quantity tomato 'pizza' sauce (see p.129)
2oz (50g) Cheddar cheese, grated
2oz (50g) wholewheat breadcrumbs

Dip the prepared aubergine slices in flour. Put into hot oil and, turning once, fry them for $\frac{1}{2}$ minute. Drain on kitchen paper and keep hot until all are fried. Heat the tomato 'pizza' sauce and pour a little into a shallow dish, cover with grated cheese and some aubergine slices. Continue layers until all are used up, finishing with tomato sauce. Cover with a mixture of brown breadcrumbs and grated cheese and put under a grill to heat through and brown on top.

Aubergine hors-d'oeuvre

Prepare the fruits in slices as above (allow about 3 large slices per person). Soak in olive oil (home-made, see p.130) and then grill. Place in a shallow dish and sprinkle with French dressing and chopped chives. Serve cold.

Avocados

Avocados are full of vitamins and minerals and they're one of the few fruits that also contain protein.

☆ *You can store ripe avocados in the fridge for up to a week, un-ripe at room temperature. If you buy them rock hard, pop them in a brown paper bag with an apple and leave in the airing cupboard for 24 hours. Result – ripe avocado.*

Chopped or sliced avocados give a bit of panache and go much further when mixed with other foods. For example, combine them with sliced tomatoes and French dressing as a starter, or use as a garnish to 'dress up' fish dishes. Mashing or puréeing is an even better way of ekeing them out. Try this sauce as a salad dressing or as an accompaniment to fish.

Avocado sauce

1 ripe avocado
5fl oz (150ml) natural yoghurt
1 dessertspoon lemon juice
Black pepper, freshly ground
Fresh parsley or chives, chopped

Remove the stone from the avocado, scoop out the flesh and mash with the lemon juice. Blend in the yoghurt and pepper. Sprinkle with your chosen herb.

Free food

Don't despise the occasional dandelion or pass by a tree covered with elderflowers, when you know you can do something with them. Learn more about foods for free.

Elderflower 'champagne'

This is one of the best and easiest sparkling drinks you can make, and costs only a few pence per large bottle. It isn't alcoholic and because I've discovered that it can be made with fresh, dried or even frozen elderflowers, it's a drink that can be made all the year round.

---

4 large heads of elderflowers, picked on a dry sunny day
Juice and thinly pared rind of 1 lemon
2 tablespoons white vinegar
1½lb (700g) granulated sugar

Place all the ingredients in a large container with 8 pints (4.5 litres) water. Stir to help dissolve the sugar, cover with a cloth and leave for 24 hours. Strain and pour into sterilised screw-top bottles that have previously held a sparkling drink. Screw on caps tightly and leave for two to three weeks before sampling so that it develops a 'fizz'. Store in a cool place. Drink within three months.

Elderflower sorbet   *Serves 4*

5oz (150g) granulated sugar
6fl oz (175ml) elderflower champagne
2 tablespoons lemon juice
1 egg white
2 tablespoons icing sugar

Put the granulated sugar and 4fl oz (100ml) water into a pan and heat gently until the sugar has dissolved. Boil for about 5 minutes until it has thickened to a syrup. Cool.

Stir in the lemon juice and elderflower champagne and pour into a container. Freeze for 1 hour until it begins to crystallise. Scrape out the mixture into a bowl and beat well. Return to the freezer for half an hour. Repeat the beating/freezing 2 or 3 times more. It's a fiddle but worth it. Finally beat the egg white until stiff and then beat in the icing sugar a little at a time. Fold this into the frozen elderflower mixture after its last beating, then return it to the freezer. Allow to soften slightly in the fridge before serving.

Pissenlit au lard

The French eat this a lot, having a bit more respect for their wild herbage than we do. They even serve it in restaurants. Dandelions are rich in minerals, so if you've a plant in your garden – cosset it! Pick the leaves from the centre of the plant when they're young and tender in the spring.

Fry a little chopped bacon gently until the fat flows. When the bacon is crisp, add it, with the melted fat in the pan, to shredded young dandelion leaves. Add a squeeze of lemon juice and toss all the items together. Grind some black pepper over the top and serve as a starter or side salad.

☆ *The perfect excuse for lazy gardeners: place a flowerpot over your dandelion plants to force them slightly and encourage young, pale green foliage.*

FRUIT

Although I always try to buy fruit in season, I'm never without apples, oranges and bananas. Apart from the dishes you can make with them, I find that a constant flow of people through the house depletes the fruit bowl. People seem to have an automatic impulse to grab as they pass by. Seems it's what the right arm's for!

The other thing I do is make an enormous bowl of fruit salad to keep in the fridge, then you're never stuck for a pud. It's one way of making your fresh fruit go further. I just chop everything roughly and pour over unsweetened orange or apple juice – no sugar needed. In the summer I make no bones about eating as many soft fruits as I can – after all they're around so briefly that it's worth the expense just for that short time. My fruit salads take on a really exotic touch then – peaches, nectarines, raspberries, even the odd kiwifruit to add a different colour. Just one, sliced thinly, makes a fruit salad look classy.

Ask your friends and neighbours if they'd be happy to barter with you – you could offer them jars of marmalade or jam in exchange for some of their fruit. Swap your gluts! Pick-your-own farms are fun and the produce is certainly fresh, but they're not always as cheap as they seem and we can't all get to one without a car. Why not try having a chat with your greengrocer and see if he'd be willing to order a tray of produce for you. He may be able to offer it to you at wholesale prices plus a little extra for his trouble. The price may well be as cheap or cheaper than pick-your-own.

Summer pudding

This is a wonderful pudding which uses all the fruits which are especially good for us, and if you have a freezer it can be made all the year round. Traditionally it's made by lining a bowl with plain white bread and filling the centre with lightly stewed fruit. This is then covered with a lid of bread and kept in the fridge under weights to be turned out the next day. Eaten with cream there's nothing better.

My version is slightly different as I use home-made wholewheat bread. I line the bowl in the same way but in the middle I layer bread and fruit till I reach the top. This way you don't need quite as much fruit but it tastes just as good. I stew the fruit in its own juices – a mixture of blackcurrants, strawberries, raspberries, or any seasonal berries or even out-of-season ones from the freezer. When all the fruit has been used up I finish with the last slice of bread. The easy way to weight the pudding is to slide on a similar-shaped container which has been filled with water. After being in the fridge overnight the whole thing is firm enough to turn out on a plate. And don't forget the cream. I find plain yoghurt really isn't quite the same with this dish, but a fruit yoghurt is a nice accompaniment.

Fruit fool

This is basically a fruit purée which is folded into a custard and cream foundation. To keep the cost down you could use all custard or mix it with some non-dairy cream. If you beat a little sweet white wine or sweet sherry in with the cream and fold in the fruit, the whole thing turns into a syllabub. The proportions are according to what you've got; allow about 5fl oz (150ml) of made-up fool per person.

My favourite fools are gooseberry, rhubarb, raspberry and strawberry. Frozen fruit can just be thawed and sieved, then folded into your custard/cream mixture. Fools made with stewed fruit need a little more care as too much juice can make the fool too runny. The end result should be the consistency of thick cream.

Bananas

You can freeze bananas but the skins go black and the flesh is mushy when defrosted. However, children love to eat them while they are still partly frozen. Peel back some of the skin and they can eat them like an ice lolly. Look out for bananas going brown – these are often sold off cheaply and make wonderful Banana bread.

Banana bread

8oz (225g) self-raising flour
1 level teaspoon baking powder
3oz (75g) butter or soft margarine
3oz (75g) granulated sugar
1 egg
1 heaped dessertspoon apricot jam
2 or 3 ripe bananas, mashed
Few chopped nuts (optional)

Sift the flour and the baking powder. Cream the fat and sugar until fluffy, add a teaspoon of the flour and beat in the egg. Fold in the remaining flour and the rest of the ingredients. Pour into a greased and floured 1lb (450g) loaf tin and bake at gas mark 4, 350°F (180°C) for about 45 minutes until golden brown and firm to the touch. (Cover with foil after 30 minutes if it's browning too early.) Turn out and cool on a wire rack.

☆ To prevent browning put foil shiny side up. To aid browning put shiny side down.

Oranges

Wonderful all year round – I'm never without them. But what about all that peel? I used to throw it away but I've discovered there's such a lot you can do with it. So whenever you eat fresh oranges or serve the following dish, have a go at some of the other 'appeeling' ideas!

☆ *To remove peel and pith easily from citrus fruit, put in a bowl and cover with boiling water. Leave for 15 minutes. Strain and peel or keep in the fridge until ready to use. This works well with those small cheap oranges where the peel is difficult to remove.*

Turkish oranges

Serves 4

4 oranges
Sugar syrup (see p.132)

Thinly pare the peel from 2 or 3 of the oranges and reserve. Then remove all the peel and pith from all the fruit. Slice each orange crossways into ½in (1cm) slices and hold the slices together with cocktail sticks in the shape of the original orange. (This is so that each person can be served with what looks like a whole fruit.) Cover the oranges with sugar syrup and leave to soak.

Cut the reserved peel into fine shreds. Bring the shredded peel to the boil in a little water, strain and repeat twice with fresh water each time. (This takes away the bitterness.) Add the shreds to the oranges in the syrup. Store in the fridge until ready to serve. A dash of home-made cream (see p.98) makes this dish a special treat.

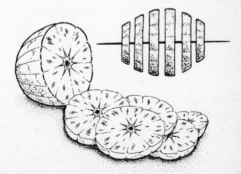

Candied peel

If you're not ready to use your leftover peel at once, pack it into polythene bags and freeze. Orange, lemon and grapefruit skins are all suitable for candied peel.

Wash the peel and simmer for 1–2 hours in water until tender. If you're using grapefruit, change the water 2 or 3 times as this removes the bitterness. Better still, you can simmer the peel in a low oven if it's on for something else, or pressure cook for 20 minutes. Drain the peel and put in a heavy pan. Cover with stock sugar syrup (see p.132) and bring to the boil. Remove from the heat and leave the peel to soak in the syrup overnight. The next day, bring it to the boil again, cool and leave overnight. On the third day, simmer until the peel has absorbed as much syrup as possible. Place the peel on a wire rack to drain. Any syrup left over can be stored in the refrigerator and used again. When the peel has dried out, store in a cool place in screw-top jars.

Chocolate orange sticks

Cut up strips of candied orange peel and dip in melted chocolate. Leave to set on greaseproof paper and store in an airtight tin. I make these as a Christmas treat.

Orange and lemon peel marmalade

6oz (175g) orange peel (approximately the peel from 2 large sweet oranges)
2.2lb (1kg) granulated sugar
Peel, flesh and juice of 1 large lemon

Chop or mince the orange and lemon peel finely and put in a large pan with 2 pints (1.1 litres) water. Leave to soak overnight. Next day, simmer slowly until the peel is soft (about 1½ hours). Measure the amount of liquid and if necessary make it up to 1½ pints (900ml). Stir in the sugar, add the lemon flesh and juice and bring to the boil. Boil rapidly for 15 minutes or until a set is obtained. (Don't expect a solid set as there's no orange flesh to give added pectin.) Leave to stand for about 10 minutes to prevent the peel from rising to the top, then pot as usual.

Note: To soften fruits quickly and to save fuel when cooking, use a pressure cooker. In the above recipe, soak the peel in $1\frac{1}{2}$ pints (900ml) water overnight, then cook at high pressure for 15 minutes to soften the peel. Turn off the heat and allow the pressure to drop gradually. Remove lid, measure the liquid and make it up to $1\frac{1}{2}$ pints (900ml) and continue as above.

Apple cake and apple scones
This old recipe uses no eggs. Originally made with all butter I've substituted some margarine. You could use all margarine but the flavour won't be as good. 'You pays your money – you takes your choice!'

12oz (350g) cooking apples
12oz (350g) self-raising flour
3oz (75g) butter
3oz (75g) margarine
$\frac{1}{2}$ teaspoon cinnamon
Milk to mix
Sugar to sprinkle

Peel, core and coarsely grate the apples. Do this immediately before using them to prevent them going brown. Sift the flour and cinnamon into a mixing bowl, rub in the fats until the mixture is like breadcrumbs, then stir in the apples and sugar. Mix with a little milk to make a firm dough. Pat flat into a square greased tin and bake at gas mark 6, 400°F (200°C) for 45 minutes. Sprinkle with sugar. When cold cut into squares.

To make apple scones, roll the dough out on a floured board and cut into rounds. Cook on a lightly oiled griddle or in a heavy frying pan until golden on each side.

Fruit sorbet   *Serves 4*

Sorbets are a cool, refreshing way to end a meal and so easy to make. If you serve them prettily in glasses or in frozen scooped-out fruit shells such as orange, grapefruit or melon, they add a party touch to any occasion.

The quantities given here will feed four. However it's worth making a bigger batch if you can. If you are using fruit with small pips, it's best to put it through a nylon sieve before using.

8oz (225g) fruit purée (unsweetened)
2fl oz (50g) sugar syrup (see p.132)
Juice of 1 lemon
2 egg whites, stiffly beaten

Combine the fruit purée, sugar syrup, 2fl oz (50ml) water and lemon juice. Put the mixture in the freezer or freezing compartment of your fridge and leave until it is just beginning to set round the edges. Whisk the mixture and fold in the stiffly beaten egg whites. Return to the freezer until set. (If you beat the sorbet 2 or 3 times before finally whisking in the egg whites you will get a smoother result.)

Almost any fruit will do but some can be a bit bland. Try adding a spoonful or two of brandy to peaches or apricots, or crushed mint leaves to gooseberries. A splash of lemon juice will pep up rhubarb, a splash of rum will do marvels for apple.

☆ *Using alcohol in cooking needn't be extravagant. Remember never to tip up the bottle and just pour. If you measure by the spoon, you'll be in control. There are 70 dessertspoons in a 70cl bottle so just divide the price of the bottle by 70.*

Plum solid

Serves 4

This is an old recipe taken from a book belonging to my
grandmother. It can be made with any kind of plum.
You can choose between flavouring with claret as they
did for the top table or almond essence which was the
below-stairs version. Depends who's coming to dinner!

1lb (450g) plums, washed and de-stalked
4oz (110g) granulated sugar
1 inch (2.5cm) long stick of cinnamon
Rind of 1 lemon, thinly peeled
1oz (25g) powdered gelatine
1 glass claret or 1 teaspoon almond essence
Flaked almonds to decorate

In a pan put the plums, sugar, cinnamon stick and lemon
rind and cover with 15fl oz (400ml) water. Simmer until
the plums are tender, then strain off the liquid and
reserve. Rub the plums through a sieve and discard the
stones and skins. Dissolve the gelatine in the warm plum
liquor, strain it into the plum purée and add the claret
or almond essence. Keep stirring until it is cold. Pour
into a mould which has been rinsed out with cold water
and leave to set. Turn out on to a glass dish and
decorate with flaked almonds. Serve with a cream/
yoghurt mixture or vanilla ice cream.

Plum charlotte

Serves 4

Another recipe from the old book and a variation on
the apple version. It is also a good way of using up
bread that has passed its peak.

Line a pudding basin with thick slices of bread and
butter (buttered side out), filling all the crevices with
crumbs. Fill up the basin with lightly stewed, drained
plums, reserving the juice. Cover the top with more
thick slices of bread and butter (they used to cut their
own bread in those days). Bake the pudding in a
moderate oven – gas mark 4, 350°F (180°C) – until the

bread is brown and crisp.

Thicken the juice with a little cornflour. To serve, turn the pudding out and sprinkle with a little caster sugar. Hand the sauce separately.

Spicy pear and meringue surprise   *Serves 4*

Make this pudding when you are cooking a meal in the oven. Put the ramekins in at least 20 minutes before you want to serve them, but they can stay in longer in a cooling oven.

---

4 ripe pears, peeled, cored and sliced in circles
12 cloves
4 dessertspoons orange juice
1 egg white
2oz (50g) sugar

Divide the pear slices between 4 individual heatproof dishes such as ramekins. Stud each one with 3 cloves and pour a dessertspoon of orange juice over each. Whisk the egg white until stiff, then fold in the sugar. Pile some meringue on to each dish, peaking it with a fork and making sure the fruit is completely sealed. Bake in the (pre-heated) oven at gas mark 3, 325°F (170°C) for about 20 minutes (or longer in a cooling oven) until the meringue is lightly browned. Serve hot.

☆ *Grate the zest from left-over citrus peel and freeze it in small quantities. Use it for flavouring cakes and puddings.*

5
DAIRY PRODUCE

Milk, cheese, eggs, butter – they're all things I mainly buy not to eat or drink as themselves but to use to create other dishes. Grated cheese bubbling on top of a dish under the grill, eggs to bind a mixture for baking or to lighten puddings by adding a whipped white, milk to make many other useful things such as yoghurt and curd cheese. Used like this, they not only go further themselves but help to make other dishes go further too. I hardly ever serve a cheese board; it's too tempting to cut off a large chunk and bingo! – your cheese ration's disappeared. But grated into quiches, flans and pizzas and used to top fish, pasta and omelettes, it goes a long, long way.

You may well find that your allowance for this section can be cut down dramatically if you start using dairy foods in this way – then you've got the happy task of deciding what to do with your savings.

Milk

Have you ever wondered what life would be like without the milkman? Yes, well ... apart from everything else, we wouldn't be able to make jokes about him! I don't think we really appreciate the service our dairies provide and if we're not careful we'll lose it altogether. Milk is cheaper in the supermarket than on the doorstep and there's a constant temptation to buy it there instead of from the daily delivery round.

But – those bottles on the doorstep don't just mean a daily supply of milk. For me they also mean yoghurt, curd cheese, cream and soured cream, all of which I can make from the milk but at a fraction of the cost of buying them separately. And if I haven't got to carry that lot home, there's more room in the shopping basket for something else. So with all those advantages I think it's worth hanging on to the daily delivery.

I buy two types of milk – skimmed for drinking and silver top which I use for making yoghurt, cream, butter and curd cheese. Once the cream (top of the milk) has been taken off silver-top, it's virtually the same as semi-skimmed. Top of the milk can be used for any recipe calling for single cream and, collected over a few days, can be whizzed in a liquidiser to make a whipped cream. If you carry on whizzing, it'll turn into butter. This is fun to do and you get the bonus of buttermilk as well which is excellent for pancakes and scones.

Some dairies don't deliver fresh skimmed or semi-skimmed milk, only offering UHT skimmed milk. This stands for Ultra-Heat-Treated and gives what I think is a rather nasty boiled taste. Now if supermarkets can supply any amount of these fresh milks, so can the dairies. Be bold and ask for it – and keep on asking.

Store your milk in a cool dark place – that usually means the refrigerator. If you leave milk in the sunlight for an hour or more it loses some nutrients as well as probably going sour on you. If you have to leave milk on a doorstep for any length of time, then invest in a bottle cooler. This is made of porous pottery which is first soaked in water and then put over the bottle. The evaporation keeps everything cool. But keep it standing in water to do the job properly. Indoors, if you haven't a fridge, a cold wet cloth (with its ends also trailing in water) placed over the bottle works just as well.

Yoghurt

Now I'm not overkeen on eating yoghurt *au naturel* unless I've stirred in some fruit or honey, but I do use it a great deal in cooking, and it's always cheaper to make it yourself. It needs a warm place to develop (I use the top of our central heating boiler), but even the special electrical kits very soon pay for themselves.

1 pint (570ml) milk
1 tablespoon dried milk powder
2 heaped teaspoons bought natural yoghurt

Heat the milk to boiling point. Boil for 1 minute and remove from the heat. Cool slightly and stir in the dried milk powder. Cool to 100°F (that's very slightly above blood heat – see tip below). Put the yoghurt into a warm basin, add a little of the milk and blend together. Then stir in rest of the milk. Cover the bowl and keep in a warm place for up to 8 hours. Once the yoghurt has set, keep it in the fridge.

Yoghurt can also be made in a wide-necked thermos or in any warm place such as the airing cupboard or a gas oven with pilot light. However, it's important that the source of heat remains constant during the setting period. Too cold and the yoghurt won't set. To hot and it curdles. To make more yoghurt, keep back 2 teaspoons and use for the next batch. After several batches begin again with fresh bought yoghurt to keep up the quality.

Testing for blood heat requires a dip in of a finger. If it feels neither hot nor cold, that's blood heat. Always remember that if a recipe calls for liquid to be blood heat, for some reason it also assumes you've got the sense to warm up the ingredients and bowl slightly. If you don't, the liquid loses heat as soon as it's mixed with the cold ingredients. But very few cookbooks tell you to do this. For this reason if everything I'm using is at room temperature, then I always make sure my liquid is a degree or two over blood heat. Common sense really, although it took me years to work it out.

☆ *An ordinary clinical thermometer is very useful for checking whether a liquid is at blood heat (98.4°F, 37°C) – keep one just for culinary purposes. Old ones will be marked in Fahrenheit, new ones in Celsius (100°F is 40° Celsius).*

Ordinary natural yoghurt is a very good alternative to cream swirled in soups, stroganoffs etc. Use the type labelled 'thick yoghurt' where you are substituting for a whipping or double cream

Wholewheat pizza
Serves 4

This is one of those quick pan-fry recipes. Once you've got the makings assembled, the whole thing can be cooked and served in 5 minutes. Unbelievable but true.

4oz (110g) wholewheat flour or granary bread flour
½ teaspoon baking powder
½ teaspoon bicarbonate of soda
Yoghurt to mix
1 tablespoon oil (home-made olive, see p.130)
Tomato ('pizza') sauce (see p.129)
Mushrooms, sliced
Grated cheese (what you can spare)
Black olives (from the home-made oil)
Bacon scraps, fried, or chopped ham (optional)

Sieve together the flour and the raising agents. Stir in enough plain yoghurt to make a soft dough. Turn out on to a floured board and roll into a thin circle to fit a large frying pan. Heat the oil in the pan, and put in the dough. Cook for ½ minute, then turn the dough to the other side, adding a little sauce, mushrooms, grated cheese, and bacon or ham if using. Decorate with halved, stoned olives. Cook for ½ minute, then place under a pre-heated grill and cook until the cheese is bubbling (about 2–3 minutes). Serve with a green salad.

A variation in flavour would be to mix chopped fresh or dried herbs or a dash of garlic purée into the dough.

Herb quiche

Yoghurt gives this quiche an agreeable sharpness to the flavour. Either use all yoghurt or half yoghurt/half non-dairy cream. This recipe uses rather a lot of herbs, but you can always use parsley and lemon balm, which tend to grow in abundance, to make up the bulk.

4oz (110g) wholewheat pastry
10fl oz (300ml) thick yoghurt
2 eggs
1 pint (570ml) jug full of mixed fresh herbs, chopped
Black pepper, freshly ground

Line a 7 inch (18cm) flan tin with the pastry. Beat up the eggs. Stir in the yoghurt and the herbs. Season with pepper and pour into the flan case. Bake at gas mark 5, 375°F (190°C) for half an hour. Eat hot or cold.

Note: Some herbs such as mint, thyme and sage are very strong in flavour. Avoid using a lot of these unless it's a taste you like. Chives, parsley, marjoram, sorrel, basil, lemon balm and tarragon are all fairly mild and go well together.

Yoghurt salad

Celery sticks, finely chopped
Walnuts, chopped
Up to 5fl oz (150ml) natural yoghurt
Black pepper, freshly ground

Mix all the ingredients together in a bowl.
This is just one of numerous yoghurt and salad combinations. Almost any crunchy, raw vegetables will blend well with yoghurt and you can flavour it with spices and fresh herbs to suit your taste.

☆ *To make mayonnaise go further, mix equal quantities with natural yoghurt.*

Yoghurt dressing

Stir the grated rind and juice of a lemon into natural yoghurt and use as salad dressing. It's particularly good with red and white cabbage, Chinese leaves, grated carrots, celery, peppers or beansprouts.

Yoghurt fruit flan

Serves 4

10fl oz (300ml) thick yoghurt
Dried fruit (sultanas, raisins, apricots)
1 tablespoon fresh mint leaves, finely chopped
8oz (225g) shortcrust pastry
2 eggs, beaten
Sugar to taste

Soak the dried fruit in the yoghurt with the mint leaves overnight. Line an 8 inch (20.5cm) flan dish with pastry. Stir the eggs and a little sugar into the fruit and yoghurt mixture and pour into the pastry case. Bake at gas mark 5, 375°F (190°C) for half an hour. Eat hot or cold.

Frozen yoghurt

Serves 4–6

1 teaspoon powdered gelatine
3fl oz (75ml) evaporated milk
2oz (50g) sugar
10fl oz (300ml) natural yoghurt
½ teaspoon vanilla essence

Sprinkle the gelatine in a little warm water to soften. In a small pan, bring the evaporated milk to just below the boil over a low heat, stirring occasionally to prevent a skin forming. Off the heat, add the sugar and the softened gelatine. Stir until the gelatine is completely dissolved and the mixture is smooth. Add the yoghurt and vanilla essence. Mix well. Cool until the mixture starts to thicken, then freeze.

This is the basic mixture to which you can add any number of tempting flavourings. Freeze the mixture for 1 hour, remove from the freezer and beat well. Stir in your chosen flavouring and return to the freezer.

Strawberry frozen yoghurt: add 4oz (110g) puréed strawberries.
Lemon frozen yoghurt: add the juice of two lemons – more if desired.
Pina colada frozen yoghurt: add 4oz (110g) crushed pineapple and grated coconut to taste.
Blackberry frozen yoghurt: add 4oz (110g) puréed fresh or frozen blackberries.
Chocolate mocha: add 1 level tablespoon instant coffee to the evaporated milk before heating, and 1 tablespoon melted chocolate, later, after beating the partly frozen mixture.

Yoghurt fruit ice cream

Serves 4

8oz (225g) puréed fresh soft summer fruit (strawberries, raspberries, black or redcurrants)
Sugar to taste
Squeeze of lemon juice
10fl oz (300ml) thick yoghurt
5fl oz (150ml) non-dairy cream
2 egg whites, stiffly beaten

If I'm using raspberries or currants, I like to put the purée through a nylon sieve to remove the pips.

Stir all the ingredients, except the egg whites, together in a large bowl and whisk with an electric whisk to incorporate as much air as possible. Freeze until the mixture begins to solidify round the edges, then fold in the stiffly beaten egg whites. Return to the freezer. Remove from the freezer at least 30 minutes before you want to eat it.

Yoghurt scones

Here's an idea for a different tea-time treat. Why not substitute a fruit flavour yoghurt for the fat and milk in your normal scone recipe? It makes very light scones. Scones are always best freshly baked so I usually make a large batch and open freeze them uncooked, bagging them up when they're firmly frozen. Then I only need to bake one or two (or three) in the oven when it's on for something else. No left-over stale scones. You can bake them straight from the freezer, but if you do, add a further five minutes to the usual baking time.

Cream

If a recipe *really* needs cream I now use one of the good cream substitutes – a non-dairy cream made with vegetable fats. It has around half the fat content of single cream, is half the price and, as long as you combine it with something which has a definite flavour of its own, you'll never detect the difference. But it's not suitable for hot dishes or soups – use yoghurt instead.

If you still want that dairy cream flavour but don't want to splash out on double cream, try this:

3oz (75g) unsalted butter
½ level teaspoon gelatine
4fl oz (110ml) milk

Melt all the ingredients together in a pan over a low heat. Do not boil. Cool to blood heat (see p.93). Blend in a liquidiser for between 30 seconds and 1 minute. Pour into a bowl, cover and leave in the fridge or a cold place. Whip up with a fork before serving.

If you want to make a pouring cream, use the same amount of butter and gelatine but add 5fl oz (150ml) milk. For added flavour, stir in a small amount of icing sugar. To extend whipping cream, beat the cream until thick, then fold in the stiffly beaten white of an egg.

Butter v. margarine

This battle has been raging on our television screens for years and I for one am heartily sick of it. No-one can kid me that anything tastes better than real butter but because we now know that it's high in that wicked stuff, saturated fat, I treat it more and more as a speciality food when I feel that nothing else will do. I always buy unsalted butter which is a bit dearer but the taste is much nicer. It's better for frying too because it doesn't burn so quickly. (I usually mix the butter with a little oil which also helps to prevent it burning.) Unsalted butter keeps longer in the freezer than salted butter – up to six months.

So what, you ask, do I put on my bread? Well, usually nothing, as it happens. I have discovered something most Europeans have known for years. If you eat really good, fresh, tasty bread with your meals, it doesn't need a thick layer of fat to make it palatable. However, I *am* married to a you-know-what man so I always have in a tub of sunflower margarine which is low in cholesterol and high in polyunsaturated fats. Beware of those products called 'low-calorie spreads' – these are not necessarily high in polyunsaturates. Instead, some of the fat has been replaced by water and consequently you can't use them for baking or frying. They're also rather an expensive way of buying water!

For special treats, I make my own garlic and herb butters. Just work in a little garlic purée or chopped herbs into softened butter. Form into a roll, wrap in old butter papers and keep in the fridge. Use a pat to fry those special omelettes or to melt over your cooked pasta.

Cheese

Cheese comes in many varieties – here I am only concerned with the best for cooking purposes. Hard cheeses, such as Cheddar, Cheshire, Leicester and Edam, are all excellent, but depending upon where you shop, there will always be variations in prices. Some supermarkets sell more than a dozen different types of Cheddar alone. The cheapest is generally the mildest. It could be worth spending a few pence more per pound and buying one with a more mature flavour and using less of it. Collect some savings to buy Parmesan in a block – this keeps for ages, can be grated fresh when you need it, works out cheaper and is far more tasty than the ready prepared. You only need to buy a tiny amount at a time.

Cheese should be stored in the least cold part of the refrigerator. Wrap it closely in film or foil to exclude the air and if you're eating it from the block bring it out an hour before you need it. Return it to the refrigerator as soon as you've finished with it.

I find the most versatile fresh cheese is cottage cheese – and often I make my own curd cheese.

Curd cheese
Makes 6–8oz (175–225g)

1 pint (570ml) milk
2 tablespoons dried milk powder
1 dessertspoon rennet essence

Heat the milk to blood heat (see p.93). Stir in the dried milk powder. Remove from the heat, add the rennet and stir thoroughly. Leave to stand until set. Cut into squares with a knife, and tip into a sieve lined with muslin standing over a basin. Tie up the corners of the muslin and suspend the bag over a basin overnight to drain off the whey. Next day transfer the cheese to a bowl and cover; it will keep in the fridge for up to a week.

If you have no muslin, use a colander lined with two layers of kitchen paper and stand it over a basin overnight. Use the whey instead of water in bread-making, or you can make it up into milk again with dried milk powder.

Pasta with curd cheese

Serves 4

6oz (175g) cooked pasta (any kind)
1 small packet (8.8oz/250g) frozen spinach
Curd cheese (see opposite)
Tomato 'pizza' sauce (see p.129)
2oz (50g) grated cheese

Pre-heat the oven to gas mark 4, 350°F (180°C). Thaw the spinach in a heavy-bottomed pan until any liquid has evaporated. Oil an ovenproof dish and put the pasta in the bottom. Mix the spinach with the curd cheese and spread on top of the pasta. Pour over the tomato sauce and top with the cheese. Cover and bake for 15 minutes. Remove the lid and cook for a further 5 minutes.

Paskha

This is a traditional Russian Easter dessert and it's essential that the curd or cottage cheese used should be very well drained and as dry as possible. An ideal container to make this in is a large (clean!) clay 4½in (11cm) diam. flowerpot lined with layers of muslin. An improvisation would be a large yoghurt carton pierced with holes down the sides and around the bottom.

12oz (350g) curd or cottage cheese, well drained
2oz (50g) unsalted butter, softened
1oz (25g) glacé cherries
1oz (25g) flaked almonds
2oz (50g) sultanas
1oz (25g) candied peel
2 egg yolks
2oz (50g) vanilla sugar
1 tablespoon thick yoghurt

Decoration:
Extra almonds and cherries

Rub the drained cheese through a sieve and beat in the softened butter. Chop the cherries and mix them into the cheese with the almonds, sultanas and peel. Beat the eggs and sugar together and fold into the mixture. Lastly stir in the yoghurt and mix everything together thoroughly but gently using a wooden spoon. Pour into the lined container (see above), fold the ends of the cloth over the Paskha, cover with a flat plate and weight down – you need about 3lb (1.4kg) of pressure. Stand, narrow end downwards, in a dish and chill for at least 8 hours – preferably overnight. Some moisture will probably drain out.

　　To serve, unfold the muslin and invert the Paskha on to a clean dish. Carefully remove the cloth. Decorate the sides and top with extra almonds and cherries. Serve alone or with slices of plain cake. It will keep for 2 or 3 days.

Spinach crêpes

This is one dish where you can guarantee the family will eat its spinach, and if the small fry are still doubtful, change the name to Popeye Pancakes.

Pancakes:
2oz (50g) plain flour
2 eggs
2 teaspoons cooking oil
12fl oz (350ml) milk
1 pack (8.8oz/250g) frozen spinach

Filling:
9oz (250g) sieved cottage cheese, well drained
1 tablespoon Parmesan cheese, grated
2 tablespoons walnuts, finely ground
Black pepper, freshly ground

Sauce:
Any tomato-based sauce (not ketchup), e.g. thick tomato soup, puréed tomato 'pizza' sauce (see p.129).

Sift the flour, add the eggs and oil and slowly stir in the milk. Beat until smooth. Heat the spinach in a heavy-bottomed pan until it has thawed and the excess liquid has evaporated. Fold into the batter. Make your pancakes using this batter in the usual way.

Mix all the ingredients for the filling together. Pre-heat the oven to gas mark 4, 350°F (180°C). Place a tablespoon of filling in the centre of each pancake, fold over the sides and roll up in parcels. Place in an oiled shallow ovenproof dish, cover and bake for 15 minutes. Serve with hot tomato sauce.

☆ Try freezing cottage cheese: this breaks down the lumps and changes the texture. Drain off the excess liquid when it has thawed and it's almost like curd cheese. Good for the above recipe.

Cheddar spread

4oz (110g) Cheddar cheese (preferably mature), grated
3 hard-boiled eggs, finely chopped
1 squirt garlic purée
1 tablespoon mayonnaise
1 tablespoon thick yoghurt
1 tablespoon fresh mixed herbs, chopped, e.g. chives,
tarragon, parsley
Seasoning to taste

Put everything into a bowl and mix well (even better, use a food processor). Chill and spread on biscuits, toast or in sandwiches.

Blue cheese soup
Serves 4

Don't buy Stilton or Danish blue specially for this recipe, but it's a good way of using up crumbled or rather over-the top cheese if you've acquired some for a special occasion.

2–4oz (50–100g) Stilton or Danish blue crumbs
1 dessertspoon oil
2 onions, chopped
½ small cauliflower, chopped
1 pint (570ml) chicken stock
1 tablespoon cornflour
10fl oz (300ml) milk
Black pepper, freshly ground
Chopped parsley

Fry the onion in the butter until soft. Add the cauliflower and fry for one minute. Pour in the stock. Bring to the boil, cover and simmer for 10 minutes. Cool, then blend or process until smooth. Mix the cornflour with a little milk and add to the purée. Stir in rest of the milk and heat gently until thickened. Stir in the cheese and parsley and season with pepper to taste. Serve hot with croutons.

Stilton dressing

Here's another delicious way of using up Stilton crumbs. Blend together 1 part milk to 2 parts thick yoghurt with a few Stilton cheese crumbs (the more crumbs, the tastier it will get). Season to taste. Use with salads and white fish, or pour over hot steamed cauliflower.

☆ *Keep small pieces of cheese unwrapped in the fridge to harden if you want to grate it very finely to use instead of Parmesan.*

Eggs

There are seven grades of eggs for us to choose from but professionals always use them by weight. If a recipe calls for 1 egg, this means a 2oz (50g) egg – in other words, grades 3–4. But the very best way to buy eggs is to get grades 6 or 7 which weigh under 1¾oz (45g). Bet you haven't seen many of those in your supermarket. And that's the point – nobody seems to want them so if you can find them, they're always far cheaper in proportion to their weight. No one has told the hens we don't buy them so they keep on laying them. Any shop which sells eggs loose on trays should be able to get them for you but you will have to be prepared to accept a whole tray. They're perfect for pickling, and one of these small ones for breakfast means a smaller yolk so less cholesterol. Weigh up the required amount for use in recipes.

If you use eggs regularly, keep them in the kitchen pointed end down so that the yolk rises up to the air bubble at the rounded end and away from the shell. (Contact with the shell makes it go stale more quickly.) Otherwise keep them in the refrigerator but always make sure you bring them up to room temperature before using. The whites beat more stiffly and the yolks won't curdle.

☆ *All recipes in this book use a 2oz (50g) egg. So use either grades 3–4 or weigh out the appropriate number of smaller ones.*

Fuel saving tips for eggs

Boiled eggs *Soft-boiled:* put the eggs in a small pan, cover with cold water and bring to the boil. Remove from the heat. Cover and leave to stand for 5 minutes. Serve.
Hard-boiled: same as above but boil for 2 minutes before removing from the heat. Leave to stand for 20 minutes then crack the shells gently and place in cold water. Leave for 10 minutes before shelling. (This method doesn't result in a blue ring round the yolk either.)

☆ *Use the cold water you boiled the eggs in for watering plants. It's full of minerals.*
To extend scrambled egg, add some fresh breadcrumbs towards the end of the cooking time.

Scrambled eggs Using a non-stick pan crack in as many eggs as you need plus an egg-cup full of milk. Season to taste and stir well with a wooden spoon over a medium heat. When it thickens, turn off the heat – it will continue to cook on with the heat of the pan for a little longer.

☆ *If you're cooking more than two fried eggs at a time put two whole eggs in the pan, then just drop in the yolks of the others. There will be enough whites to go around your yolks and you can use the leftover whites to make meringues (see p.109), fold into sorbets (see p.88) – or make fritter batter (see opposite).*

Fritter batter

1 dessertspoon cooking oil
4oz (110g) plain or self-raising flour
1 egg white, stiffly beaten

Stir the oil into the flour and add enough tepid water to make a thick batter. Leave to stand for 1 hour, then fold in the stiffly beaten egg white. Use to coat pieces of fruit (e.g. bananas, apple rings) and deep fry.

Yorkshire pudding

Traditionally this was served alone with gravy as the first course of a meal. It helped to fill a few corners and meant you could get away with serving a smaller second course. Serve with the re-heated gravy kept back from a casserole.

Lard or dripping
2 eggs
1½oz (40g) flour
2fl oz (50ml) milk

Pre-heat the oven to gas mark 8, 450°F (230°C). Put a little lard into either a small square tin or a Yorkshire pudding tin with 4 individual rings. Place this in the oven to heat.

Beat the eggs into the flour and stir in the milk and 2fl oz (50ml) water (or you can use ½oz (10g) dried milk powder and all water). When the lard is smoking hot pour the batter into the tins and cook on the top shelf for 15–20 mins until the pudding has turned brown and is crispy. Turn on to a plate and fill the centre with hot gravy. Eat as a first course (they are quite large). If made in one tin cut into four before adding gravy.

Oeufs St Germain

In cooking, the term *St Germain* means any dish made with a thick purée of peas. The way to make it for this recipe is exactly the same as for Lettuce soup (see p.66). Go easy on the lettuce and add plenty of peas and a lot less stock. But there's absolutely no reason why you couldn't use any vegetable purée and give it another name.

Vegetable purée
1 hot soft-boiled or poached egg per person
Triangles of toast
Bacon bits, crisply fried and drained (optional)

Heat the vegetable purée and pile a serving on to each hot plate. Top with a shelled soft-boiled egg. Garnish with toasted triangles of bread and (optional) snippets of fried bacon.

Spanish omelette   *Serves 4*

---

1 tablespoon oil (preferably olive oil, see p.130)
1 large onion, finely chopped
A squirt of garlic purée
Approx. 4oz (110g) cold cooked potatoes, chopped
4 eggs
Black pepper, freshly ground

Heat the oil in a frying pan and add the onion and garlic. Cook slowly until the onion has softened. Add the potatoes and heat through. Break the eggs into a basin, add a little cold water and pepper. Beat lightly with a fork. Pour the eggs on top of the other ingredients in the pan and cook until the underneath is firm and golden brown. The top will still be runny. Put the pan under a hot grill to set the top of the omelette. Slide the omelette flat on to a hot plate. Serve with crusty bread and a salad.

Kipper not-quite-kedgeree

6oz (175g) long grain rice
6oz (175g) kipper fillets
3 eggs, hard boiled
1 dessertspoon sultanas
1 tablespoon mayonnaise
1 tablespoon natural yoghurt
Pinch of curry powder
Black pepper, freshly ground

Boil the rice and poach the kipper fillets. Chop the kipper fillets into small pieces and quarter the eggs. Mix together the mayonnaise and yoghurt and add the curry powder. Combine all the ingredients together in a pan and heat through gently. Serve with a salad.

Chantilly cream/soft scoop ice cream

This is one of the most amazing creams with a variety of uses. All you need are egg whites, sugar, water, cream of tartar and non-dairy cream. There are 3 stages:

1 Meringue Beat 3 egg whites with a pinch of cream of tartar until stiff. Boil 8oz (225g) sugar and 8 dessertspoons of water to the soft ball stage. This takes about 2 minutes and you test it by dropping a little of the syrup into cold water. It should mould into a soft ball. Pour the sugar mixture slowly over the egg whites and beat for some time until the mixture is solid. You can then use half the mixture to cook as meringues or pavlovas. Use the other half for the next two stages.

☆ *To store meringues, put them while still warm in polythene bags and keep in airtight tins. They'll keep for ages.*

2 Chantilly cream Beat 5fl oz (150ml) of non-dairy cream till it thickens and fold in the remaining half of the meringue mixture. This can be used to fill cakes, profiteroles etc. or to make stage 3.

3 Soft-scoop ice cream Freeze the chantilly cream and you will find it turns into a rich, soft-scoop ice cream to which you can add any of the following flavours.

Peppermint: add a few drops of peppermint essence to the cream.

Lemon: add a few drops of lemon essence to the cream.

Peanut: fold finely chopped unroasted, unsalted peanuts into the cream.

Chocolate: melt 1oz (25g) plain chocolate and fold into the cream.

Ginger: grate preserved stem ginger and fold into the cream.

Rum and sultana: soak sultanas overnight in a little rum and stir them into the cream. A few drops of rum flavouring will give it an extra boost.

Fruit sauces
Stew the fruit of your choice (gooseberries, blackberries, plums, damsons, apricots, raspberries, rhubarb, etc.) in a little water with sugar to taste. Sieve or liquidise the fruit. Chill and serve over the ice cream, sprinkled with chopped nuts.

Soufflé of prunes *Serves 4*

6oz (175g) dried prunes
Orange juice or cold (black) tea
3oz (75g) caster sugar
4 egg whites, stiffly beaten
Non-dairy cream, whipped

Soak the prunes overnight in the orange juice or cold tea. Then cook them in the liquid (made up to 10fl oz

(300ml) with cold water) until tender. Pre-heat the oven to gas mark 5, 375°F (190°C). Drain, stone and chop the prunes very finely and mix in the sugar. Beat the egg whites until stiff and fold into the prunes. Pour into a greased ovenproof soufflé dish and bake for 10–12 minutes. Serve immediately.

Redcurrant whip   Serves 4

Grated rind and juice of $\frac{1}{2}$ lemon
2oz (50g) caster sugar
1 tablespoon redcurrant jelly
2 egg yolks

Put all the ingredients in a heatproof bowl with 3fl oz (75ml) water. Place the bowl over a pan of hot water and beat until the mixture has thickened. Remove the heat, stand the bowl in cold water and continue to beat until cool. It will thicken further. Serve in 1 large dish or in 4 wine glasses.

6
GROCERIES

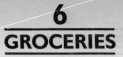

The store-cupboard is the nerve-centre of your kitchen – get this bit right and you'll be able to cope in any emergency. And lists are important here. When stocks begin to run low, put them on a list and add to it anything else you need before you go out. But don't panic if you *do* run out of one thing – you'll always be able to manage with something else. Half the fun of cooking is discovering what you can make from almost nothing.

Stocking up

Weight for weight large packs can often work out cheaper than small ones (but check first – there could be a damaged pack or a small size on special offer). Prices also vary from store to store so it's wise to 'comparison shop' before purchasing. You can save pounds this way. But do remember that there's no point in buying large packs if you don't use that item often. Although sugar and rice keep almost indefinitely, most products deteriorate with time.

Not every basic item needs to be bought as quite a number can be manufactured at home without much effort. It's always interesting comparing costs of home-made versus bought – sometimes the difference can be amazing. If there's little difference I don't see much point beavering away unless home-made is very superior in taste. There's never time to do everything and it's far better to spend what time you have on the best money-savers.

It's a pretty safe bet, for instance, that all home-made biscuits, preserves and cakes will get eaten at the gallop, but when offering up something new it's best to get the family involved at the outset. Experiment on a small scale – there's less to throw away then if things don't work out. Run tasting sessions, expect criticism, let them suggest improvements. But never make gallons of anything unless they approve. Money can only be saved if the end product is used.

Not so long ago I took all food for granted, never realising that this blinkered me as to its possibilities. I always obeyed everything that was written on a packet and never thought of adapting a recipe to suit my needs.

Then I ran out of money, out of rice and out of pasta and was forced to make my own lasagne *for the very first time*. The thrill of providing something I didn't have to go out and buy (ignoring the fact the ingredients were paid for a week or two previously) led me on to exploring and experimenting. This was great fun – the family couldn't understand why we were eating better meals (this always happens when you think a bit more about what you are doing) and money began to be saved. But none of this could have happened if I hadn't a few basic ingredients to hand. Since then I've learned how to get the best value from them. This is my choice for a starter-kit store-cupboard – if you've got this lot, you can add your own favourite products and you'll be fire-proof.

Starter-kit store-cupboard
Grains
Flour: plain white, wholewheat, strong plain flour, cornflour.
Rice: easy-cook (long grain and risotto), brown rice.
Pasta: spaghetti, shells and spirals. Lasagne. (Also look out for wholewheat and green pastas.)
Assorted: porridge oats, bulgar (cracked wheat), pearl and pot barley.

Dried pulses
A good assortment. Begin with haricot, butter, and red kidney beans, red and green lentils, split peas.

Cans

Tomatoes, tomato purée, baked beans.
Tuna, mackerel, pilchards, sardines.

Herbs, spices and seasonings

As wide a variety as possible. Whole black peppers and
nutmegs to grind freshly. Family's favourite sauces,
relishes and ketchups. Tabasco and Worcestershire to
add zing. Garlic purée. Dry English mustard. Vinegar.
Wine concentrate.

Oils and fats

Sunflower oil, unsalted butter, polyunsaturated
margarine, vegetable fat.

Sugars and syrups

Granulated and muscovado sugar. Honey. Golden syrup.
Black treacle.

Fruit and nuts

Sultanas, dried apricots, prunes. Peanuts (unsalted),
walnuts, flaked almonds.

Miscellaneous

Instant dried yeast powder, powdered gelatine, raising
agents. Cake mixes. Cooking chocolate. Popcorn. Seeds
for sprouting. Dried milk. Tea and coffee.

☆ *It's much cheaper to use loose tea than teabags. The
tea leaves can go on the garden as compost!
If you use real coffee, save the dried used grounds
to stuff pin-cushions – the pins won't go rusty.*

GRAINS

Flour

With *plain flour* and raising agents you can make your
own self-raising flour. Just add 2 level teaspoons of
baking powder to 8oz (225g) of plain flour. (If you're
making scones or eggless cakes, add 4 level teaspoons
of baking powder.) When baking cakes, always sift
the flour to incorporate as much air as possible, so
don't bother to buy 'superfine' or 'supersifted' flours.
Do it yourself, it's better and cheaper.

Raising agents are basically bicarbonate of soda and
cream of tartar. You can buy these ready mixed as
baking powder but I always like to have the other two
as well because you sometimes need the extra 'lift'. You
can also make your own baking powder.

---

1 level teaspoon of bicarbonate of soda
2½ level teaspoons of cream of tartar
½ teaspoon cornflour
equals
4 level teaspoons of baking powder

Wholewheat flour is the best flour of all for most things.
Look out for bags labelled '100% stoneground'. This
means it is the pure, natural flour, unbleached and with
no added chemicals and the wheatgerm oil is evenly
distributed through the flour.

Strong, plain flour is used in breadmaking. If I don't want
an all-brown loaf, I sometimes mix wholewheat and
strong white flours to make a 'half-and-half' loaf.

Cornflour is not normally used as a flour but as a
thickening agent for sauces. But I sometimes substitute
1oz (25g) cornflour for flour in a cake to give a finer texture.

To this basic list, you may like to add some different
flours: *rye flour* to make rye bread, or *buckwheat flour*
to make buckwheat pancakes. There are many different

kinds of flour available, all with subtly different tastes. It's fun experimenting with them. Don't forget the recipe for bread on p.14 and, once you've made it, try the recipe for bread and butter pudding opposite.

Bara brith

This Welsh fruit loaf is incredibly easy to make. Traditionally it is always cut into very thin slices so one loaf will keep going for some time. Keep it tightly wrapped in foil between servings.

8oz (225g) sultanas
2oz (50g) candied peel, chopped (see p.86)
8oz (225g) plain flour
8oz (225g) wholewheat flour
1 teaspoon mixed spice
2 teaspoons sugar
1 sachet instant dried yeast powder (see p.137)

Put all the ingredients into a bowl and mix well. Add 15fl oz (400ml) hand-hot water and mix into a dough – you can add more flour or water if necessary to achieve the right consistency.

Knead well for 10 minutes on a lightly floured board and put into one greased and floured 2lb (1.1kg) loaf tin. Cover and leave to rise until doubled in size. Bake in the oven at gas mark 3, 325°F (170°C) for about 40 minutes. Remove from the tin and put back on the shelf for a further 5 minutes. Cool on a wire cake rack, then wrap in foil.

☆ *Bread freezes very well, so if you bake your own, make a double batch and put the surplus in the freezer. If you buy your bread, it's cheaper to buy one large loaf than two small ones. So if you can, buy a large loaf, cut it in two and put half in the freezer. Well wrapped in polythene bags, it keeps for six months.*

Bran bread pudding

6 slices wholewheat bread
10fl oz (300ml) orange juice (unsweetened)
2oz (50g) sultanas
1 dessertspoon honey
2 eggs, separated
1 teaspoon ground cinnamon
Nutmeg, freshly grated
½oz (10g) butter

Break up the bread into small pieces, mix with the orange juice and sultanas and leave to soak for several hours.

Beat up the egg yolks with the honey and stir into the bread mixture. Stir in the spices. Whisk the egg whites until thick and fold into the mixture. Pour into an ovenproof dish which has been well greased with some of the butter. Dot the top with the remaining butter.

Bake in the oven at gas mark 3, 325°F (170°C) for half an hour or until set.

Pancakes are one of the cheapest 'basics' but you can turn them into a feast. They can be rolled, folded, parcelled, cut into strips like pasta, baked, fried, layered – turned, in short, into a multitude of sweet and savoury dishes.

Basic pancake batter

1oz (25g) dried milk powder
1 egg
4oz (110g) plain flour
1 teaspoon vegetable oil (optional)

Mix the dried milk powder with 10fl oz (300ml) water. Whisk in the egg and beat in the flour. Leave the batter to stand in a cool place for about 1 hour. Stir in the vegetable oil just before cooking. Wipe over the frying-pan with kitchen paper dipped in oil and heat the pan. Pour in enough batter to coat the pan thinly and cook quickly until golden brown underneath. Turn and cook the other side. You will have to re-oil the pan every so often. Keep the cooked pancakes warm by piling them up on a warm plate in a low oven.

Try folding in some thawed and drained frozen spinach to the batter (see p.103). This gives you lovely speckled pancakes to which you can add savoury fillings: cottage cheese and walnuts, chopped cooked chicken and bean sprouts, chopped ham and sweet corn – the combinations are endless.

Make your pancakes with different flours – wholewheat pancakes are tasty and so are buckwheat.

Try sweet fillings too, e.g. curd cheese mixed with the grated rind and juice of an orange and cinnamon. Sprinkle caster sugar and cinnamon on top.

Rice

I expect you're wondering why I've chosen to buy 'easy-cook' and brown rice – both more expensive than the standard plain white rice.

First the 'easy-cook' rice – I buy this because it's *foolproof* (no glutinous lumps of rice which the family won't eat) and because it's been treated in a way which means it retains more nutrients than ordinary white rice.

Secondly the brown rice – this is much the best because, like wholewheat flour, the whole goodness of the grain is retained. It does take longer to cook, but because it's so filling, you'll probably eat smaller helpings.

Cooking method: The basic rule for cooking all rice is 1 measure of rice to 2 measures of water.

White rice: bring the water to a fast boil, pour in the rice, stir once, bring back to the boil, cover and reduce the heat. Peek just once to make sure the liquid is at a slow boil and then do not remove the lid again. After 10 minutes, remove from the heat and leave to stand for a further 10 minutes. Take off the lid, fluff with fork and cover with a tea towel. Rice will keep hot like this for up to half an hour.

Brown rice: add to cold water, bring to the boil, stir and cover. Reduce the heat and simmer for 15 minutes. Then leave to stand for 20 minutes. This method saves up to 15 minutes cooking time.

Risotto   *Serves 4*

8oz (225g) easy-cook Italian (risotto) rice
Cooking oil
1 pint (570ml) chicken stock
Mushrooms, chopped
1 onion, chopped
Celery stump, grated
Peas, nuts, sultanas to taste
A little white wine (optional)
Parmesan cheese, freshly grated
Black pepper, freshly ground

Heat a little oil in a large saucepan. Fry the rice in it gently and add the wine. Pour in the stock and cook until the rice is tender. (You may need to add more stock or water if all the liquid is absorbed before the rice is cooked.) Fry the mushrooms, onion, celery and peas in a little more oil. Stir in the nuts and sultanas. When these have heated through, combine with the rice and sprinkle with freshly grated Parmesan cheese and black pepper. This can be eaten hot or cold, and you can also stir in chopped cooked chicken.

You can make this recipe with a mixture of other grains too which produces an interesting variety of flavours and textures. Begin with the one which takes the longest to cook and then add the others:

allow 1 hour for pot barley
     45 minutes for pearl barley
     20 minutes for bulgar
     20 minutes for rice

☆ *Try to save any liquid left over after soaking or cooking grains. It's full of nutrients and can be used in soups, sauces and gravies.*

Pasta

Spaghetti is the cheapest form of pasta, but some shapes like shells and spirals hold a sauce well. As well as the ordinary kind you can also buy wholewheat and spinach green. Home-made pasta is very well worth making, as for one thing it take far less time to cook. Make up batches of pasta dishes for the freezer.

Fuel-saving cooking method for dried pasta: Put the pasta into plenty of boiling water and add 1 teaspoon of oil. Stir, then reduce the heat and simmer for 2 minutes. Remove from the heat. Cover with a towel and a lid. Leave to stand for a further 10 minutes, and drain. This methods saves up to 10 minutes cooking time.

Pasta salad

Serves 4

8oz (225g) cooked pasta shapes (shells or spirals)
4oz (110g) pineapple (canned or fresh), cut into slivers
Few red and green pepper strips
2 medium tomatoes, cut into chunks
French dressing
1 teaspoon made mustard
1 dessertspoon mint, chopped

Mix together the pasta, pineapple, peppers and tomatoes, blend a little French dressing into the mustard, pour over pasta mix and toss lightly. Sprinkle with mint and serve. This is a good base to which to add a little cubed cooked meat, such as ham, chicken or lamb. Alter the herb according to the meat. If in doubt, use parsley.

Quickie spaghetti

This is a recipe for any number of people from one up – just use as much of each ingredient as you like.

2oz (50g) spaghetti per person
Cooking oil
Onion, chopped
A squirt of garlic purée
Bacon bits, diced
Green vegetables, chopped (e.g. leek, courgette, pepper)
Mushrooms, chopped
Parmesan or Cheddar cheese, grated
Black pepper, freshly ground

Cook the spaghetti. Meanwhile heat the oil and stir-fry the onion, garlic, bacon, vegetable and mushrooms until the bacon is crisp and the vegetables still crunchy (see p.54). Mix with the drained hot spaghetti and sprinkle with the cheese and black pepper.

Lemon tuna with pasta   Serves 4

8oz (225g) pasta, any sort
1 can (7oz/200g) tuna
1 onion, chopped
Cooking oil
1 tablespoon lemon juice
10fl oz (300ml) chicken stock
1 teaspoon made mustard
3 teaspoons cornflour
1 tablespoon milk (top of the milk if you have it)
2oz (50g) Cheddar cheese, grated
Black pepper, freshly ground

Cook the pasta. Meanwhile, drain the tuna and fry the onion gently in the oil till soft. Add the lemon juice, stock, mustard and flaked tuna. Mix together the cornflour and milk, stir into the mixture until it simmers and thickens. Remove from the heat, add the cheese and stir till it melts. Pour the sauce over the drained hot pasta and grind some black pepper over the top.

Assorted grains

Porridge oats Oats contain a high percentage of protein and so are good to use as 'extenders' to meat dishes. They also make nourishing bread, pastry, biscuits and cakes. Porridge oats can be turned into oat flour using a grinder or liquidiser.

Bulgar This is a pre-cooked wheat product. All you need to do is soak it in water or stock. It's useful for extending casseroles and as an alternative side dish to rice, and is the basic ingredient for Tabbouleh (p.123).

Pearl and pot barley Pot barley is the unprocessed grain – pearl barley has been processed. Although pot barley has all the good bits left on, it's usually cheaper than pearl barley. It's available in some supermarkets and health food shops. Again, barley is a useful extender for meat dishes and makes a thick nourishing soup when combined with vegetables.

Muesli
So many bought varieties of muesli have sugar and salt added that it's well worth making your own – and, naturally, cheaper.

All you need is porridge oats, nuts and dried fruits which you can mix together in the quantities you prefer. Chop up the nuts and fruit, but not too finely. I like to add in wheat flakes as well, and also liberal amounts of roasted sesame and sunflower seeds. To roast these seeds, just shake them in a dry pan over a medium heat until they turn golden brown. Serve the muesli with milk or yoghurt or chopped fresh fruit.

Oatcakes

1½oz (40g) vegetable fat or dripping saved from making beef stock
8oz (225g) fine oatmeal or grind your porridge oats

Pre-heat the oven to gas mark 6, 400°F (200°C). Melt the fat. In a bowl combine the oatmeal, fat and a small amount of boiling water to bind. Knead the mixture in the bowl and turn out on to a board sprinkled with oatmeal. Roll out thinly and cut into rounds or triangles. Place on a greased baking sheet and bake for 5–10 minutes or until crisp. Cool on a wire rack. Serve with cheese or honey.

Note: Don't forget you can cook oatcakes in the heat of a cooling oven (see pp.9–10).

Tabbouleh

Serves 4

3½oz (85g) bulgar
15fl oz (400ml) chicken stock
2 tablespoons fresh parsley or coriander, finely chopped
2 tablespoons chives, finely chopped
Juice of 1 lemon
Black pepper, freshly ground
2 tablespoons olive oil (home-made, see p.130)
2 tablespoons mint, finely chopped
Lettuce leaves

Put the bulgar in a bowl and stir in the chicken stock. Cover and leave to soak for about 1 hour. Drain in a sieve, pressing out as much liquid as possible. Put the drained bulgar in a clean bowl and add the parsley, chives, lemon juice and pepper. Toss gently with a fork. Just before serving, add the oil and mint and toss again.

Serve on lettuce leaves as part of a salad, a starter or at a buffet party.

Mediterranean salad   *Serves 6–8*

2oz (50g) bulgar
10fl oz (300ml) chicken stock
8oz (225g) frozen green beans
1 can (7oz/200g) tuna, drained
3 firm tomatoes, skinned and diced
4 tablespoons fresh parsley, chopped
2 tablespoons mayonnaise
1 tablespoon thick yoghurt
2 tablespoons olive oil (home-made, see p.130)
2 tablespoons lemon juice
Black pepper, freshly ground
Crisp lettuce leaves

In a large bowl mix the bulgar with the stock. Cover and leave to soak for 1 hour. Drain well through a sieve, pressing out the excess liquid. Cook the green beans, drain and cool. Place in a bowl with the bulgar, add the flaked tuna and all the remaining ingredients except the lettuce. Mix well together. Line a shallow dish with lettuce leaves and pile on the bulgar mixture. Serve at once or chill to serve later. In the Middle East it is traditional to use the crisp leaves to scoop up the bulgar mixture and eat it with the fingers. Good for *al fresco* eating.

Lemon barley water

4oz (110g) pearl barley
4 lemons
4oz (110g) sugar
Slices of lemon to decorate
Ice cubes

Put the barley in a pan, just cover with water and bring to the boil. Drain, rinse with cold water and return to the pan. Cover with 2 pints of cold water and bring to the boil. Cover and simmer for 1 hour.

Peel the rind from the lemons as thinly as possible using a potato peeler, and squeeze the juice. Strain the barley liquid into a jug, add the sugar, lemon rind and juice. Stir well and leave to cool.

Strain and pour into sterilised screw-top bottles. Store in the fridge and dilute as required. Serve with ice cubes and slices of lemon.

☆ *The left-over barley can be added to a soup or casserole, or frozen away to be used later.*

Pulses

These are all packed with protein so a *must* for any store-cupboard. There's an enormous variety and each has its own flavour. They keep for ages but the older they are the longer they take to cook so keep them turning over. The best plan is to keep them on view so that you're reminded you've got them.

Cooking method: Soak the dried beans overnight in plenty of water. Tip into a saucepan and bring to the boil. Boil rapidly for 10 minutes to neutralise any toxins, then cook very slowly until the beans are tender. The time will vary with the type and age of the pulses. Add more water if necessary. Alternatively, once you have fast-boiled them for 10 minutes, the beans will take 1 hour or more in a casserole in a slow oven and at least 3 hours in a slow cooker on low (but longer won't hurt). Never add salt as this prevents them from softening.

☆ *Cook large batches of pulses, drain well and toss in oil. When cold spread on baking sheets and freeze. Then bag up and use as required in chillis, salads etc. Ready-cooked beans in cans cost more than twice as much as buying dried beans and cooking them yourself.*

Pasta e fagioli   *Serves 4*

Cooking oil
1 onion, chopped
1 squirt garlic purée
8oz (225g) red kidney beans, cooked
8oz (225g) white beans, cooked
1 can (14oz/400g) tomatoes
2 tablespoons Parmesan or Cheddar cheese, finely grated
1 tablespoon fresh oregano (or marjoram) and basil, chopped, or 1 teaspoon dried
4oz (110g) pasta spirals (dry weight)
2 or 3 cooked garlic sausages (the long thin variety), sliced

Cook the pasta and drain. In a little oil gently fry the onion until soft, stir in the garlic purée, kidney and white beans and tomatoes with their liquid. Add the herbs and bring to the boil. Simmer for 5 minutes to develop the flavour. Put the pasta and sliced sausage in a casserole and add the bean mixture, stirring gently to mix. Cover and bake at gas mark 4, 350°F (180°C) for 20 minutes. Remove the lid, top with the grated cheese and bake uncovered for a further 10 minutes until the cheese is bubbling.

The Goode cassoulet

Serves 4–6

Cassoulet is a classic dish based on pork and chicken meat, but I like to make it with whatever I have left over: ham or gammon, pork chop or pork shank, chicken winglets. The garlic flavour is a must, though. The best way is to use the thin garlic sausages, but, failing this, add a generous squirt of garlic purée.

8oz (225g) haricot or butter beans, soaked overnight
1 pint (570ml) chicken stock
1 pork shank (or see above)
Chicken pieces (winglets etc.)
2–4 cooked garlic sausages (the long thin variety), sliced
1 carrot, thinly sliced
1 onion, thinly sliced
1 dessertspoon clear honey
1 small can (2.25oz/65g) tomato purée, or 2 frozen cubes (see p.128)
2 slices bread, crumbed
2 dessertspoons fresh mixed herbs, chopped, or 1 teaspoon dried
1 bay leaf
Black pepper, freshly ground

Drain the beans and simmer for 1 hour in the chicken stock. Drain, reserving the liquid. Place layers of beans, pork, chicken, sliced sausage, carrots and onions in a casserole. Mix together the honey, tomato purée and the reserved bean stock. Pour into the casserole. Cover and cook for 1½ hours at gas mark 2, 300°F (150°C). Remove the lid and top with the breadcrumbs, herbs and pepper. Cook for a further hour. Serve from the pot.

Red lentil soup   *Serves 4*

1½ pints (900ml) chicken stock
6oz (175g) red lentils
1 onion, chopped
Cooking oil
1 level teaspoon ground cumin
Black pepper, freshly ground

To serve:
Wholewheat bread
1 lemon

Bring the stock to the boil. Wash the lentils and add to
the stock with all but 1 dessertspoon of the onion.
Reduce the heat and simmer for about 30 minutes or
until the lentils are soft. Heat the oil and fry the
remaining onion gently with the cumin for about 10
minutes until soft and golden. Purée the soup in a
liquidiser or rub through a sieve, then return to the
saucepan and heat through. Add the onion and the
cumin mixture and season to taste. Serve with
wholewheat bread and lemon wedges.

Canned foods

The canned foods I would never be without are
tomatoes and tomato purée. Watch out for special
offers on tins of tomatoes (they're usually sold three or
six in a pack) and stock up.

☆ *Large cans of tomato purée work out much cheaper*
than tubes. So buy a large can and freeze the purée
in ice cube trays. When frozen, you can pack the
cubes in polythene bags to store and use as much as
you need straight from the freezer.

Tomato 'pizza' sauce

This is a must for pasta dishes and pizzas. You can store it covered in the fridge for up to a week, or, if you have a freezer, make it in bulk and freeze in small yoghurt cartons.

---

2 tablespoons oil
1 medium onion, chopped
1 can (14oz/400g) tomatoes
1 small can (2.25oz/65g) tomato purée, or 2 frozen cubes (see opposite)
1 dessertspoon each of fresh basil and marjoram, chopped, or $\frac{1}{2}$ teaspoon each, dried
Bay leaf
1 teaspoon sugar
Black pepper, freshly ground

Heat the oil and fry the onion for a few minutes until transparent. Add the roughly chopped tomatoes, together with their liquid. Mix in the tomato purée and herbs and stir well.

Add the sugar and pepper and simmer for about 30 minutes. Remove the bay leaf, pour the sauce into a bowl, and when cool, cover and keep in the fridge.

This sauce will see you through many an emergency. It is used in the following recipes in this book:

Chicken 'n' Cheese Pancakes (p.43)
Aubergines in Tomato Sauce (p.78)
Wholewheat Pizza (p.94)
Pasta with Curd Cheese (p.101)
Spinach Crêpes (p.103)

Canned fish is another great stand-by. For recipes, see pp.37, 38, 121 and 124

Herbs, spices and seasonings

Always keep your herbs and spices in the dark to preserve flavour and colour. Pretty though the spice and herb racks are, they're no good for the contents. But there's no reason why you shouldn't have one for decoration – mine is purely for show and holds food colourings. Personal choice will decide which ones you keep in stock but the wider the variety, the tastier the meals can be.

Purists may throw up their hands in horror at my preference for garlic purée rather than fresh garlic. But I became so cross at having to throw away cloves that had gone mouldy before I could use them, I decided to give it a try, and I can honestly say I think the flavour is just as good. A tube isn't cheap, but it lasts for ages and you can use as little as you want. (Hands up all those who've used half a clove of fresh garlic because the recipe said so and left the other half to rot in the vegetable basket!) Of course, if you use garlic regularly enough not to have this problem, just substitute a fat crushed clove for one of my squirts!

Oils and fats

It is unwise when buying cooking oil to go for a really cheap oil. Not only can it be smelly, but if it's just labelled 'vegetable oil' you don't really know what's in it.

The best ones for flavour and health reasons are sunflower, corn and soya oils. And of course olive oil tastes wonderful - but it's expensive.

Use these oils rather than butter, lard or 'unspecified' margarine whenever possible – it's those 'good guys' the polyunsaturated fats again as opposed to the 'baddies', the saturated fats.

Olives in oil If you can't afford olive oil, here's a way round it. Professionals may cringe at this but it's a super way to make your own olive-flavoured oil.

Buy a few black olives, put them in the bottom of a jar and cover with sunflower oil. The oil preserves the olives and the olives flavour the oil. Use the olives for pizzas and salads and the oil for dressings and frying.

Sugars and syrups

Buy granulated only and turn it into caster sugar by whizzing it in a liquidiser. Turn the caster sugar into icing sugar by grinding in a coffee grinder. Dark brown muscovado sugar is unrefined and has a lovely treacly taste. This is a must for some marmalades, biscuits and gingerbread.

Keep a separate jar of white sugar with a vanilla pod in it. This makes vanilla sugar which you can use in ice cream, custards and other sweet dishes.

Honey is expensive but you don't usually need to use much at a time. Supermarkets' own brand is usually the cheapest, though you may prefer to pay more for a better flavour. See p.132 for a home-made version.

An economical marzipan

This, I find, is far cheaper to make than the traditional almond paste and is easier to handle, being less sticky. In fact I prefer it.

8oz (225g) icing sugar
2oz (50g) caster sugar
2oz (50g) ground almonds
1 teaspoon golden syrup
2 drops almond essence
1 egg white

Nice and easy – put everything in a bowl and mix it together. Knead until smooth. Keep wrapped in a poly bag if you're not going to use it immediately.

Sugar syrup

2.2lb (1kg) granulated sugar
1¼ pints (700ml) water

Heat the sugar and water slowly in a thick saucepan until the sugar has dissolved. Bring to the boil and simmer for 4 minutes. Cool and store in sterilised bottles in the fridge. Use for sorbets and candied peel.

Fondant icing

Special occasions like birthdays and anniversaries call for special cakes. Then I like to use this fondant icing because it's so easy to handle. This version is very similar to the real thing but is not pure white because of the syrup. However, it does take a drop of food colouring perfectly.

8oz (225g) icing sugar
½ an egg white
1 teaspoon golden syrup

Put 6oz (175g) icing sugar in a bowl, make a well in the centre and add the egg white and syrup. Mix well then turn out on to a big plate with the remaining icing sugar. Knead until all the sugar has been worked in and the fondant is smooth. You may need to add a little more sugar – it's never easy to divide an egg white in half!

Parsley honey

Here's an old farmhouse recipe which makes 1½lb (700g) of what looks and tastes exactly like clear honey for a fraction of the cost.

4oz (110g) parsley (leaves and stalks)
1lb (450g) granulated sugar
1 heaped tablespoon thick honey

Wash the parsley and put it in a big pan with $1\frac{1}{2}$ pints (900ml) water. Bring to the boil and simmer for 30 minutes. Strain through a sieve into a measuring jug. You should now have 1 pint (570ml) of liquid – if not add more water. Return the liquid to the pan. Add the sugar and bring to the boil, stirring all the time, then leave at a rolling boil for 20 minutes. Add the honey and stir until it dissolves. Remove from the heat and pot in small, hot, sterilised jars.

Marmalade

I can never see the sense of buying and preparing Seville oranges when you can get them in cans ready prepared to make up your own marmalade at no extra cost. These tins make up to 6 or 7lb (2.7–3.2kg) of marmalade.

Don't be afraid to make up your own variations. Strain some through a sieve to make a shredless jelly. Add the left-over shreds to the next jar to make a 'chunkier' marmalade. You can substitute a little muscovado sugar for the white to make a darker 'Oxford' type, or you can include the juice and peel of a lemon to give yet another flavour. Whatever you choose to do it's at least half the price of a branded marmalade. There's also a recipe for making marmalade from left-over peel on p.86.

Dried fruit

My preference is for sultanas because they are so much plumper and juicier than raisins. I always use these when a recipe calls for raisins, but obviously it's a matter of choice. Sultanas go in curries, salads, rice, breads, yoghurts, cakes and biscuits. Dried prunes and dried apricots are also 'essential stock' for me.

Prune bread

5oz (150g) dried prunes
1 level teaspoon bicarbonate of soda
1 tablespoon soft margarine
4oz (110g) sugar
1 egg
8oz (225g) wholewheat flour
1 level teaspoon baking powder
2oz (50g) chopped nuts

Soak the prunes overnight in 8fl oz (225ml) boiling water and the bicarbonate of soda. (If you are using the 'no-soak' prunes, you need only soak for 10 minutes.)

Drain the prunes, reserving the soaking liquid. Remove the stones and chop the prunes coarsely. In another bowl, cream together the margarine, sugar and egg. Sift the flour with the baking powder and add to the creamed mixture. Stir in the prunes, soaking liquid and nuts. Mix well.

Grease and flour a 1lb (450g) loaf tin and spoon in the mixture. Bake at gas mark 2, 300°F (150°C) for 1 hour. Remove from the heat and leave for 5 minutes, then turn out on to a wire rack. When cold, wrap in foil. Keep for a day before eating.

Apricot and carrot jam   *Makes 4lb (1.8kg)*

There is little difference in cost between bought and home-made apricot jam using a standard recipe. However this version is far cheaper to make because of the carrots which are undetectable. This is one of those secrets worth keeping to yourself.

8oz (225g) dried apricots, roughly chopped
8oz (225g) carrots, grated
1 orange
2 large lemons
2lb (900g) sugar

Soak the apricots overnight in $1\frac{1}{2}$ pints (900ml) of water. Bring to the boil and simmer for 30 minutes until soft. Meanwhile put the grated carrots in a pan with 10fl oz (300ml) water, the grated rind and juice of the orange and lemons. Chop the lemon shells into large pieces and add them to carrots to extract the pectin from the pith. Bring to the boil and simmer for about 1 hour until carrots are soft. Remove the pieces of lemon shell. Put the carrots and liquid into a liquidiser or processor and whizz to a purée. Put into a pan with the apricots and their soaking liquid, add the sugar and heat gently until the sugar has dissolved. Bring to a full rolling boil until setting point is reached (about 20 minutes). Pot in the normal way in hot, sterilised jars. For even more economy, use fewer apricots and more carrots.

Nuts

Peanuts are excellent value. Buy them plain, not ready salted, then you can use them in a wide variety of recipes – salads, casseroles and as crunchy toppings for flans. They are also good in coleslaw, risottos and stir-fry dishes. Walnuts are good in salads too.

Nuts go rancid quite quickly but they will keep up to 3 months in the fridge. However, I keep them in the freezer where they will last indefinitely.

Peanut butter

1 cup unsalted peanuts, shelled
1–2 tablespoons vegetable oil

Put the peanuts and oil in a liquidiser or processor and blend until you have crunchy or smooth peanut butter, according to which you prefer. Store in a screw-top jar in the fridge for up to 2 months.

Savoury peanut crackers

Makes 4 dozen

1 egg
4 dessertspoons natural yoghurt
1oz (25g) peanut butter
8oz (225g) plain flour

Pre-heat the oven to gas mark 4, 350°F (180°C). Beat the egg with the yoghurt and peanut butter until smooth. Add the flour and work to a smooth dough. (Add a little more yoghurt if necessary.) Roll out *very thinly* on a floured board and cut out circles or squares. Place on ungreased baking sheets closely (they don't spread) and prick with a fork. Bake for 12 to 15 minutes until golden. (Or place in an oven which has been pre-heated to gas mark 6, 400°F (200°C). Turn out the heat and leave for 45 minutes before removing.)

This is a very versatile recipe which you can adapt to make different savoury crackers. Use 1oz (25g) melted butter instead of the peanut butter and add the flavouring of your choice. Choose from:

Parmesan cheese
mixed herbs
garlic purée
freshly ground black pepper
sesame seeds

Peanut cookies

Makes about 2 dozen

8oz (225g) unsalted peanuts
2 eggs, well beaten
3 dessertspoons flour
Pinch of baking powder
Vanilla essence to taste
4oz (110g) soft light brown sugar

Pre-heat the oven to gas mark 5, 400°F (200°C). Grind the peanuts in a liquidiser. Beat the eggs and sugar together. Sift the flour and baking powder together and add to the eggs. Add the vanilla essence and ground peanuts. Mix well. Drop teaspoonsful on to oiled baking sheets and bake for about 10 minutes.

Miscellaneous

Yeast The new instant dried yeast powder makes light work of any bread and bun making. All you have to do is include it as one of the ingredients and just add hand-hot liquid. There are about three brands available – full instructions are given on the packet.

Gelatine Far more use than packet jelly although that can have its place. Useful in mousses, fresh fruit jellies and frozen yoghurt (see p.96).

Popcorn

This is such fun to make I never see any point in buying it ready popped. But be warned – NEVER remove the pan lid until you are sure it's finished its pops otherwise you'll have the lot all over the floor. Popping corn is available in most supermarkets, but avoid the small packs, it's far cheaper bought by the pound. If you can't get this in supermarkets, try health food stores.

You need two tablespoons of corn to 1 dessertspoon of cooking oil. Put the oil in a pan and place over a medium heat. When the oil is hot add the corn, give it a shake to coat, put on the lid and sit back. Wait for the popping to start, give the pan a shake from time to time and when the popping has ceased remove from the heat. Tip the corn into a bowl and remove any that hasn't popped. You can either leave it plain (boring but good) or toss it in melted butter, syrup or treacle. You need about 1 tablespoon of syrup or treacle for each tablespoon of unpopped corn. For a savoury party snack, toss in garlic-flavoured butter.

7
AND NOW—ENJOY IT!

After preparing and cooking food comes the presentation — sometimes the most important part of the whole thing. It doesn't matter how cheap the ingredients, if it *looks* good not only do you get the urge to eat it, but it can give the impression of being a quite luxurious dish.

Twenty minutes after we have started a meal the appetite centre in our brain is satisfied. Not a lot of people know that. So if you're a fast eater, you eat more. The trick is to serve at least three small courses rather than two large ones. (This may seem to be a chore but it needn't be if you prepare at least two of them ahead of time.) You have only to remember the small portions you get in restaurants compared with what you usually serve at home to realise you can get away with less. Then there's often a long wait between courses. The tendency, at the end of the second course, is to feel quite satisfied and quite often we do without the sweet things. Overall we haven't actually eaten that much. But it's quite rare to feel we haven't had enough. That's because it's taken more than twenty minutes to eat it. We can also steal some ideas from restaurants about presentation. A tiny plate of food or a small bowl of soup looks much more if served sitting on another slightly larger plate.

What's more, don't try to serve everyone first and then rush through your own meal ready to be up and serving the next course when everyone else has finished. Serve everything in large bowls and let them help themselves.

Food is special and important. You've spent time and effort preparing it, so it's only right it should be given some respect. Make an occasion of a meal and everyone, including the cook, will enjoy it all the more.

INDEX

142

Conversion tables

All these are *approximate* conversions, which have either been rounded up or down. In a few recipes it has been necessary to modify them very slightly. Never mix metric and imperial measures in one recipe. Stick to one system or the other.

Weights	
½oz	10g
1	25
1½	40
2	50
3	75
4	110
5	150
6	175
7	200
8	225
9	250
10	275
12	350
13	375
14	400
15	425
1lb	450
1¼	550
1½	700
2	900
3	1·4kg
4	1·8
5	2·3

Volume	
1fl oz	25ml
2	50
3	75
5 (¼ pint)	150
10 (½)	300
15 (¾)	400
1 pint	570
1¼	700
1½	900
1¾	1 litre
2	1·1
2¼	1·3
2½	1·4
2¾	1·6
3	1·7
3¼	1·8
3½	2
3¾	2·1
4	2·3
5	2·8
6	3·4
7	4·0
8 (1 gal)	4·5

Measurements	
¼ inch	0·5cm
½	1
1	2·5
2	5
3	7·5
4	10
6	15
7	18
8	20·5
9	23
11	28
12	30·5

Oven temperatures		
Mk 1	275°F	140°C
2	300	150
3	325	170
4	350	180
5	375	190
6	400	200
7	425	220
8	450	230
9	475	240

Imperial spoon measures have been used in many recipes. These are *level* spoonfuls unless otherwise stated. If you prefer to work in metric, use the following equivalents:

teaspoon = 5ml measuring spoon
dessertspoon = 10ml measuring spoon
tablespoon = 15ml measuring spoon